DETROIT

······· *in* ·······

WORLD WAR II

GREGORY D. SUMNER

GREG
SUMNER

THE
History
PRESS

Published by The History Press
Charleston, SC
www.historypress.net

Back cover: A B-24 Liberator, the 6,000th produced at Ford's Willow Run plant, on a shakedown cruise over downtown Detroit. *Courtesy Yankee Air Museum.*

First published 2015

Manufactured in the United States

ISBN 978.1.46711.947.4

Library of Congress Control Number: 2015948818

For Franklin and Eleanor Roosevelt, Edsel Ford, Rose Will Monroe, Joe Turner, Walter Reuther, Ray Bredell, Fred Logan, Joe Louis, Frank Moody, Edward R. Murrow, Hank Greenberg, Earl Zimmer

and untold others who, by their sacrifice, won the war and left us a better world.

CONTENTS

Acknowledgements   7
Introduction: Forging Thunderbolts   9

PART I: PRODUCTION
Boom and Bust   21
Accepting the Challenge   23
Big-ness   27
"A Good Drive!"   33
Rosie and Friends Go to War   39
"Bomber City?"   46
A Union Label in Berlin   52

PART II: THE MILITARY MOTOR CITY
Message from the Past   57
"Dim Those Lights!"   58
Warriors in Our Midst   64
Their Stories Are Finished   68
Telenews   71
Fighting Jim Crow in Uniform   75

PART III: EVERYDAY LIFE IN THE ARSENAL OF DEMOCRACY
Open All Night   81
At the Movies   87

Contents

Enemy Agents?   92
"Spontaneous Combustion"   94
Making Do with Less   104
"Hi-Yo Silver!"   114
"Hitting One Against Hitler"   118

PART IV: VICTORY!
A War "Half-Won"   127
"Reconversion"   135
Reverberations   141

Selected Bibliography   155
Index   157
About the Author   160

ACKNOWLEDGEMENTS

I want to express my deep appreciation for the professionalism and care of the staff at The History Press in bringing this project to life, especially Greg Dumais, Elizabeth Farry and Magan Thomas. I can never thank all the other people who helped along the way, but let me name a few: John Baxter, Casey Blake, Ron Carpenter, Chris Causley, Matthew Church, Cindy Dashnaw, Gerry Doelle, Patrick Doran, Roy Finkenbine, Michael Hauser, Chad Hickox, Charles Hyde, Yassine Johri, Renee Kettering, Donald Kroger, Gary Lichtman, Dave Nicholson, Julie Osborne, Maryrose Patrick, Robert Rouse, Jim Wheeler, ReShawn Wilder and Mike and Karen Wilhelm.

Introduction

FORGING THUNDERBOLTS

"We must be the great arsenal of democracy."

So declared Franklin Roosevelt in one of his landmark "fireside chats" from the White House on December 29, 1940. The United States was not yet formally at war, but he understood well the magnitude of the threats gathering abroad. Indeed, at that moment the very survival of democracy seemed uncertain. "Never before, since Jamestown and Plymouth Rock, has our American civilization been in such danger as now," the president told an audience he knew to be filled with skeptics.

Across the Atlantic only Great Britain, its resources dwindling by the day, held out against the Nazi *Blitzkrieg* that had swept through western Europe earlier in the year. Should England fall, FDR warned, "all of us, in all the Americas, would be living at the point of a gun." Hitler's bombs were raining down on London even as he was speaking. It was the worst attack of the war, designed to blunt any morale boost those who stayed up until 3:00 a.m. might have taken from the broadcast.

The situation on the other side of the world was equally grim. Black-and-white *March of Time* newsreels brought home the slaughter of civilians as Hirohito's war machine ruthlessly imposed its will on Manchuria. Newsboys on street corners across the country shouted one another down with the latest bad headlines.

More than 100 million were tuned into Roosevelt's message that Sunday evening, carried coast to coast on over five hundred stations. Many were accustomed to relaxing at that hour every week with the Jack Benny program. But this was not a night for frivolity. Bars and restaurants closed early, and movie houses and theaters stayed dark. According to police blotters, even criminals took the night off to take in what the president had to say.

FDR delivered his words with a calculated mix of alarm and reassurance. The task before him was formidable: preparing his fellow citizens for a war they did not want but that was sure to come anyway. "Frankly and definitely there is danger ahead—danger against which we must prepare. But we well know that we cannot escape danger by crawling into bed and pulling the covers over our heads."

Roosevelt went on to explain that the nation's vast resources, above all its industrial capacity, had to be harnessed and applied with the greatest force if there was to be any chance of reversing the Fascist tide. He called now for more courage, more sacrifice, more speed and more production.

No city rose to the challenge with more vigor than Detroit.

To be sure, polls showed that the majority of people in southeast Michigan, and in the country at large, remained opposed still to American involvement in foreign conflicts. The bitter experiences of the First World War were still fresh. The president's opponents condemned his run for an unprecedented third term in 1940 as a power-grab and assailed his policy of "Lend-Lease" aid to Britain as recklessly provocative.

"America is now in danger of being dragged down the river a second time," a *Detroit News* reader insisted just weeks before the "arsenal of democracy" speech. The previous spring, thousands assembled on Belle Isle for the sunrise dedication of the Nancy Brown Peace Carillon, named in honor of a longtime *News* columnist. The nickels and dimes they donated for its construction were an expression of hope that the young men now coming of age might be spared yet another round of senseless bloodshed. Women in the crowd carried signs saying, "Mothers Will Not Lend or Lease Their Sons."

"Isolationist" sentiment remained strong for a full year after FDR's address. Father Coughlin of Royal Oak's *Shrine of the Little Flower*, famous for the anti–New Deal screeds he broadcast from the studios of WJR Radio every week, had by this time been removed from his radio pulpit, but there were plenty of other figures wary of "Roosevelt the Dictator" and his flirtations with war. By far the most prominent was Detroit-born Charles Lindbergh, the featured speaker at America First rallies around the country.

There *were* Detroiters calling for action against the Axis, especially among those most directly connected to the suffering abroad. Members of the Jewish community in the northwest part of the city had for years

"Mothers Will Not Lend or Lease Their Sons." With memories of World War I still fresh, "isolationist" sentiment was strong in the early 1940s. *Courtesy Walter Reuther Archives, Wayne State University.*

been blanketing representatives in Washington with appeals that *something* be done to slow down the Nazi reign of terror. Residents of Polish Hamtramck hanged Hitler in effigy from lampposts when the Germans overran their ancestral homeland in September 1939, as did the eastside Belgians when Brussels and Antwerp fell in 1940. And elders in Detroit's small Chinatown organized marches to bring attention to Japanese atrocities in Asia. The interventionists were, however, distinctly in the minority.

Although his hands were substantially tied, Roosevelt nevertheless took steps to bolster the nation's anemic army, navy and air corps at an accelerating pace after the swastika was hoisted over the Eiffel Tower. In 1940, he convinced Congress to authorize the country's first-ever peacetime draft, requiring men between twenty-one and thirty-five to register for possible military duty. Surviving by a single vote the next year, the conscription bill added bulk to the armed forces, lately so starved of funds that infantry recruits trained with Springfield bolt-action rifles that had not been fired since the doughboys laid them down in 1918.

They launched salvos of flour at cardboard tanks and hurled eggs instead of hand grenades. General Patton ordered and paid for some of the hardware needed by his mobile armored units from the Sears/Roebuck catalogue.

The United States ranked *nineteenth* in the world in fighting capability on the eve of its entry into World War II—just behind Romania. After the fall of France, army chief of staff George Marshall gave the president and his cabinet this sobering assessment of the situation: "If five German divisions landed anywhere on the [east] coast, they could go anywhere they wished."

FDR knew he needed all the help he could get to prepare the country for war, and he acted with skill and judgment in recruiting the right people for the right jobs. His first move was to ask General Motors president William Knudson to plan and coordinate a crash munitions program. "Big Bill," a devoutly anti-Roosevelt Republican, put aside political differences and said yes. He would be the most indispensible of the "Dollar-a-Year-Men" in Washington, captains of industry who donated their time and talents to the nation's defense.

Under Knudson's guidance, the vast industrial *potential* of the United States edged toward becoming a *reality*. Factories, foundries and steel mills just emerging from the Great Depression roared back to life to fill orders for war goods. With retooling, they added shifts and hired new workers by the tens of thousands. Lend-Lease shipments to Britain and, after it was invaded by the Nazis in June 1941, the Soviet Union reinforced the drive to maximize production. "Give us the tools," Winston Churchill had declared, somewhat wishfully, "and we will finish the job."

The shock of December 7, 1941, ended in one blow any illusions that the United States could remain aloof from the fight. Every Detroiter old enough to take notice would forever remember where they were and what they were doing when the first bulletins came across the radio that fateful Sunday.

To be honest, most civilians had never *heard* of Pearl Harbor and, if pressed, could not locate it on a map. Teenager Fred Herr's response was typical. Working his usual matinee shift in the balcony of the Hollywood Theater that afternoon, he was startled from a half-doze when another usher bounded up the stairs, two or three steps at a time, to break the news. Fred recalled his puzzlement: "He said Japan had attacked Pearl Harbor, and I said, 'Who the hell is Japan?' We weren't too up on our foreign affairs at the time. I was sixteen. I just thought if it was such a big deal, why didn't they make an announcement in the theater?" By nightfall, everyone knew that Pearl Harbor meant war and that life as they had known it was about to change dramatically.

It didn't take long for the human cost to register. A Western Union telegram from the secretary of the navy arrived a few days later at the Grosse Pointe home of Ben Marsh Jr., a seaman serving on the USS *Arizona*, notifying the family that he was among the 2,403 lost in that ghastly raid. Ensign Marsh was Detroit's first official casualty.

Even after 9/11, it is hard for us to imagine the fear—bordering at times on hysteria—that gripped the American psyche in the aftermath of the Japanese haymaker. With it came coordinated attacks on the Philippines and other archipelagoes in the western Pacific, driving unprepared Yanks and Brits back at every turn. And four days after the attack in Hawaii, Hitler honored his mutual aid pact with Japan, declaring war on the United States. The Axis was united and on the march. Some wondered, with good reason, if perhaps the war was *already* lost.

"Wake Island Has Fallen." "Battleship *Omaha* Still on Fire." "Hong Kong Now in Jap Hands." "Moscow Under Nazi Siege." The picture was uniformly bleak. Newspapers published color maps of the Americas overlaid with concentric circles to mark the projected range of enemy bombers.

This was unfamiliar territory for a people used to the security of two vast oceans. From San Diego and Seattle to Boston, Philadelphia and New York, it registered that the world had all of a sudden become dangerously smaller. Invasion rumors spread unchecked even in Chicago, Detroit and other landlocked cities—the more sensational, the greater the speed. Telephone switchboards jammed with reports of Japanese *Zeroes* on the horizon as citizens anxiously turned their eyes skyward.

	Name	Rate	Name	Rate	Name	Rate	Name
SMic	R. N. KING, JR.	ENS	F. E. MALECKI	CT	I. J. MURPH[...]		
CGM	F. W. KINNEY		J. S. MALINOWSKI	SMic	J. G. MYERS	SKic	
Sic	G. L. KINNEY	QM2c	H. L. MALSON	SK3c			M. J. QUARTO
CWT	W. A. KIRCHHOFF	Sic	E. P. MANION	S2c	E. H. NAASZ	SF2c	J. S. QUINATA
SKic	T. L. KIRKPATRICK	CAPT	A. C. MANLOVE	ELEC	A. J. NADEL	MUS2c	
Sic	E. KLANN	SOic	W. E. MANN	GM3c	J. G. NATIONS	FC2c	N. J. RADFORD
GM3c	R. E. KLINE	GM2c	L. MANNING	S2c	"J" "D" NAYLOR	SM2c	A. S. RASMUSSEN
S2c	F. L. KLOPP	GM3c	R. F. MANSKE	Y2c	T. D. NEAL	Sic	G. V. RASMUSSON
COX	R. W. KNIGHT	EM3c	S. M. MARINICH	COX	C. R. NECESSARY	Sic	W. RATKOVICH
ATT2c	W. KNUBEL, JR.	Sic	E. H. MARIS	Sic	P. NEIPP	S2c	G. D. RAWHOUSER
Fic	W. E. KOCH	Sic	J. H. MARLING	S2c	G. NELSEN	SC2c	C. J. RAWSON
[US2c	C. D. KOENEKAMP	Fic	U. H. MARLOW	COX	H. C. NELSON	Sic	H. J. RAY
Sic	H. O. KOEPPE	SCic	B. R. MARSH, JR.	ENS	H. C. NELSON	BMic	C. REAVES
Sic	B. KOLAJAJCK	Sic	W. A. MARSH	Sic	L. A. NELSON	CTC	C. C. RECTOR
HAic	A. J. KONNICK		T. D. MARSHALL	S2c	R. E. NELSON	F3c	J. J. REECE
Sic	J. A. KOSEC	BM2c	H. L. MARTIN	Y3c	A. R. NICHOLS	Sic	J. B. REED, JR.
S2c	R. KOVAR	Sic	J. A. MARTIN	BMic	B. A. NICHOLS	Sic	R. E. REED
T2c	J. D. KRAMB	MSMTHic	J. O. MARTIN	S2c	C. L. NICHOLS	TCic	P. J. REGISTER
'S2c	J. H. KRAMB	Sic	L. L. MARTIN	F3c	L. D. NICHOLS	S2c	J. M. RESTIVO
Sic	R. R. KRAMER	GM2c	B. D. MASON	S2c	G. E. NICHOLSON	EM3c	E. A. REYNOLDS
Sic	F. J. KRAUSE	Sic	C. H. MASTEL	S2c	H. G. NICHOLSON	Sic	J. F. REYNOLDS
)X	M. S. KRISSMAN	S2c	D. M. MASTERS	GM3c	T. J. NIDES	EMic	B. R. RHODES
	R. W. KRUGER	QM2c	C. E. C. MASTERSON	PHMic	F. T. NIELSEN	CM3c	M. A. RHODES
sc	A. L. KRUPPA	Sic	H. R. MATHEIN	BMKRic	R. H. NOONAN	Sic	W. A. RICE
ic	H. H. KUKUK	Sic	C. H. MATHISON	Sic	T. J. NOWOS[...]		

USS *Arizona* memorial, 2015. Ensign Ben Marsh Jr. of Grosse Pointe was among the 2,403 who perished as a result of the Japanese attack on December 7, 1941. *Courtesy Robert Rouse.*

The West Coast was, of course, most vulnerable to a follow-up attack. As a precaution, Rose Bowl officials moved their traditional New Year's Day football game from Pasadena to Duke University's stadium in Durham, North Carolina. In the weeks and months after Pearl Harbor, all kinds of security measures were taken, some prudent and well-executed and others rash, ineffective and—in retrospect at least—downright foolish. In any case, the authorities had their hands full maintaining public calm.

Fear was not the only reaction in that wounded moment, however. There was also a deep sense of outrage, tinged with overtly racial overtones. The ferocity of the sneak attack caused many to conclude that the Japanese were beasts worthy of nothing less than complete annihilation. And the news from Hawaii also, paradoxically, brought with it a sense of *relief*. At least now the hand-wringing tensions of "neutrality" had been broken.

Eleanor Roosevelt went ahead with her regularly scheduled Sunday evening radio broadcast just hours after the assault. In her familiar patrician voice, firmer and more resolute than usual, the First Lady set the tone, reassuring listeners of her faith in the "free and *unconquerable* people of the United States." It was a masterly two and a half minutes, filled with the words "we" and "our":

> *For months now the knowledge that something of this kind might happen has been hanging over our heads. And yet it seemed impossible to believe, impossible to drop the every-day things of life and feel that there was only* one *thing which was important: preparation to meet an enemy, no matter* where *he struck. That is all over now, and there is no more uncertainty. We know what we have to face and we know that we are ready to face it.*

Before signing off, Mrs. Roosevelt paused to speak directly to the wives and mothers in the audience. With sons in the service, she knew the burdens they were now being asked to bear. And she reminded everyone on the homefront of their heightened responsibilities: "We must go about our daily business more determined than ever to do the ordinary as well as we can."

Personal plans were put on hold, animosities were suspended and a unifying sense of purpose burned off the fog of confusion. "There is no room for disagreement when American lives are blotted out and our own soil is violated," declared the *Detroit Free Press*, up to then a vigorous opponent of intervention. "Whatever superficial divisions there may have been were settled with steel by Sunday's events."

At noon on December 8, the president put his stamp on the event, vowing to Congress that the nation would "win through to total victory," no matter how long it might take or how bad things appeared to be in the short term. Most welcomed the fact that it would be a team effort. "[E]clipsing the long, painful road ahead," historian Geoffrey Perrett has written, "was the deep satisfaction derived from a new sense of community. Something of a family feeling prevailed."

Even as the first reports from Honolulu were being digested, army and Federal Bureau of Investigation officials, in partnership with local law enforcement, moved to beef up security at Detroit's large manufacturing plants and other potential targets for sabotage or even air strikes. The *Free Press* offered this bare-bones account of the steps taken to protect the border with Canada:

> *Four truckloads of Selfridge Field troops arrived in the city at a late hour to set up guard at the Ambassador Bridge and the Detroit-Windsor Tunnel. Similar precautions were planned for the Michigan Central railroad tunnel and the vital car-ferries. The Detroit Police, meanwhile, broadcast a notice requesting that all scout cars, cruisers and patrolmen closely watch radio stations and radio transmitter areas.*

By dawn of the first full day of war, the line at the army induction center on Fort Street snaked all the way around the block. A shortage of doctors slowed down the initial processing, and many applicants were rejected for poor health, their thin frames and damaged teeth a legacy of the Depression. Those who made it past the first hurdle soon found themselves standing in the cavernous waiting room at Michigan Central, duffel bags over their shoulders, saying tearful goodbyes as they began the journey to training camps scattered in the four corners of the country.

For many, this would be the first real trip away from family, friends and the comforting points of reference they had taken for granted since childhood. A St. Christopher's medal, a rabbit's foot or some other talisman would, they hoped, ward off the dangers they were bound to face. A wallet photo or two reminded them of whom they had left, fueling many a dream about home.

Over the next four years, 200,000 Detroiters would serve in uniform, in every branch of the military and in every theater and battlefront of the war, on land, at sea and in the air. More than a few would never make it back.

Virtually every industrial enterprise in Detroit converted its operations to meet the national emergency, from the most humble tool-and-die shop to the

Naval recruits. Induction centers in Detroit opened to long lines the morning after Pearl Harbor. *Courtesy Reuther Archives.*

gigantic auto plants. Instead of making cars, the mass-production genius for which the city was famous would from now on be devoted to the manufacture of planes, tanks, jeeps, half-tracks, trucks, marine and aircraft engines, artillery pieces, machine guns, mortar shells and bullets—*lots* of bullets. With the Motor City leading the way, the United States would produce 44 *billion* rounds of small-arms ammunition for the soldiers at the front.

Admiral Isoroku Yamamoto, the reluctant architect of Japan's Hawaii gambit, warned his superiors in Tokyo about the risks they were taking in the ambush of America's Pacific fleet. As a young man, Yamamoto had studied in the United States, and he knew something about the psychology of its people. In the 1930s, he had written, "Anyone who has seen the factories in Detroit and the oil fields in Texas knows that Japan lacks the national power for a naval race with America."

The smoke had yet to clear from the decks of the crippled ships along Battleship Row and the dead were still being recovered from their watery graves, but Yamamoto suspected already the ruin that would come to his nation because of its aggression. The war would have to be a short one, or

Japan's defeat was almost certain. "I fear all we have done," he confided to an aide, "is to awaken a sleeping giant and fill him with a terrible resolve."

In size and impact, the results of the wartime drive for production would be staggering, and the Motor City's contributions would dwarf those of other industrial centers. A large proportion of the tanks used in North Africa and Europe were built locally by Chrysler, Ford and GM. In four short years, the modest McCord Radiator and Manufacturing Company on East Grand Boulevard stamped out twenty million steel combat helmets for Allied soldiers on all fronts.

"Like England's battles would be won on the playing fields of Eton," UAW leader Walter Reuther would observe, "America's can be won on the assembly lines of Detroit." On the last night of his Teheran summit with FDR and Churchill in 1943, Marshal Joseph Stalin—not one to dispense praise lightly—lifted his glass to the city for its role in winning the new kind of warfare pioneered by the Nazis, a struggle of "machines against machines."

Detroit was transformed like no other metropolitan area in the nation. Within its flat, 138-square-mile expanse, the population swelled with migrants from farms and small towns in Michigan and the throughout the middle west. Thousands more, white and black, came up from the hardscrabble South, bringing with them their culture and their traditions, as well as their prejudices. "These two groups were obliged to work side-by-side in the war plants," Maya Angelou wrote of boomtown life during these years. "Their animosities festered and opened like boils on the face of the city."

The newcomers jostled with the natives over jobs, housing, recreational space and just about everything else—in a society, it must be remembered, still ruled by "Jim Crow" segregation. Conflict inevitably erupted in Detroit, to the point of a devastating race riot. As heartbreaking as the carnage was, it at least forced people to reexamine the ideals for which they were fighting. "Master race" thinking was a lot less defensible once America entered the fight against Hitler. The war contained seeds of reform that would mature into the civil rights revolution of the next generation.

Through all of the frictions and frustrations, the job of munitions production went on, a tribute to the architects and engineers of the Motor City and the men—and women—who labored around the clock in their factories. The "can-do" spirit of those days we often talk about was not just mythology or propaganda. Those who lived through that era recall a very specific kind of electricity in the air, part patriotic fervor, in part the welcome novelty of full lunch pails and money in the pocket.

Detroit's residents adapted with amazing speed to the new conditions, when change and restless movement were the only constants. People worked hard and then relaxed at movies and saloons and dance halls, Tigers games and all-night bowling alleys. They piled onto buses and streetcars, prayed in churches and synagogues, looked after neighbors, took on boarders, "made do with less," stood in lines, bought war bonds and raised victory gardens. To be sure, some evaded their responsibilities or sought to profit from the crisis. But they did not reflect the attitudes and behavior of the overwhelming majority.

All of this frenzied activity was "normal" for the children of Detroit, who, after all, knew no other way of living. They were too busy snapping up comic books at the drugstore and buying candy at the movie theater concession stand to notice the surrealism of wartime. Parents may have disapproved of the violence they consumed so avidly in the Saturday afternoon serials—innocent, of course, by today's standards—but they handed over the money for them to go nonetheless. On weekdays, youngsters raced home from school to catch their favorite radio programs. They followed the war's progress with stickpins on maps and transformed the grim business of air raid drills and scrap drives into fun and games.

In an essay for the *New York Times Magazine* of January 10, 1943, J.L. Duffus tried to capture in words the dizzying new world he had observed during a trip around America's industrial heartland:

> *Against the night sky are the chimneys of great factories. Lights ablaze.*
> *Machinery roars and thunders. A Democracy at war has its troubles and*
> *its weaknesses. But the work gets done. And this is Detroit…a city amazed*
> *and often confused, but a miraculous city, a city forging thunderbolts.*

PART I

PRODUCTION

*Out of enormous rooms
armies will roll and fleets will fly.*

−Time *magazine cover story on Detroit industry and the war, March 23, 1942*

BOOM AND BUST

Detroit has always been known for the drive and rough-hewn practicality of its citizens, set against the often violent swings of a boom-and-bust economy. "[N]ot so long ago," the 1940 WPA *Guide to Michigan* noted of the city's genteel, turn-of-the-century ambience, it was a tree-shaded small town "unobtrusively going about its business of brewing beer and making carriages and stoves. Bulky Georgian mansions frowned over iron fences on Woodward and Jefferson Avenues." In those days, residents claimed, with some justification, that theirs was "the most beautiful city in America."

Then came Ford and Buick, Durant and Olds, the Dodge and Fisher brothers—the auto barons who, in a few short years, transformed Detroit into an industrial powerhouse the likes of which the Victorian-age elders could scarcely recognize, let alone understand. During the First World War and the Roaring Twenties that followed, the city prospered beyond even the barons' dreams, and its international profile soared. The symbol was Ford's Model T, embodiment not only of simplicity and moral rectitude but also of leisure and endless mobility.

The Motor City set the pace in other ways, too. Prohibition stimulated a law-defying entrepreneurial spirit, and the local economy saw the rise of the largest bootlegging operation in the country. Through ingenuity and brute force, the "Purple Gang" and its imitators smuggled in oceans of alcohol from the Hiram Walker Distillery just across the mile-wide Detroit River in Windsor, Ontario.

In 1929, it all crashed—harder and faster than anywhere else. Images of cigarette-smoking flappers and speakeasy decadence gave way to breadlines, shuttered factories and labor violence.

By 1940, a new war was engulfing Europe, and orders for military hardware (as well as automobiles and other consumer items) picked up dramatically. Unemployment all but disappeared. How long would *these* good times last? No one could say for sure. "Detroit is still in the formative stage of its development," the WPA *Guide* advised readers in search of solid ground and a reliable sense of the future. "There is nothing final about it, nothing fixed."

But with their talents for improvisation, the city's polyglot citizens would endure, no matter what came their way. And as hard as life might be, there were always consolations. "Detroit has little of the quaint, the bizarre, the picturesque," the *Guide* conceded, and its people no longer bragged about its aesthetic appeal. Still, even in the shadow of refinery flames, steel mills and "grimly functional factories" it retained its sacred spaces, its moments of poetry and grace. A few scenes revealed this more human side: "the Gypsy restaurants in Delray to the south, the Eastern Market (one of the few places in the city where horses are seen after daybreak) and the carnival on Paradise Valley's Hastings Street after a Joe Louis victory." That they were so hard to find made them all the more precious.

ACCEPTING
THE CHALLENGE

We must raise our sights all along the production line," Franklin Roosevelt declared in his State of the Union address of January 1942. FDR went on to propose a series of goals so ambitious that many dismissed them as pie-in-the-sky. Sixty thousand planes a year? Forty-five thousand tanks? Twenty thousand antiaircraft guns? "Let no man say it cannot be done," the president thundered, his jaw set as he stood locked into his heavy leg braces. "It *must* be done. And we have undertaken to *do* it!"

Roosevelt aimed his words at every boardroom and shop floor in the country. But they were also a shot across the bow of the Axis leadership, where skepticism about the nation's capabilities was almost an article of faith. "Americans only know how to make refrigerators and razor blades," Hitler's *Reichsmarschall* Herman Goering scoffed with his usual arrogance.

Soon enough, Goering would have to eat his words. It was Yamamoto who had it right: the sleeping giant was awake, and the national resolve was taking shape. Maybe FDR's numbers weren't so fanciful.

The federal government looked to the Midwest for a disproportionate share of the munitions needed to conduct a war on two fronts. A foundation of infrastructure was already in place there, and it was farther removed from danger than the coasts. With 4 percent of the nation's population, the state of Michigan would receive 10 percent of the defense contracts awarded between 1942 and 1945, the lion's share going to Detroit and its environs.

Manufacturers in the Motor City responded to the president's call to arms in diverse and creative ways. Decisions were often made with input from the bottom up, as befitting a democracy at war. A full year before Pearl Harbor, engineers from 1,500 area machine shops were invited to the Graham-Paige plant downtown to examine a disassembled heavy bomber. They determined the parts they could make most efficiently, and bids followed accordingly.

Not all local enterprises involved in munitions work were from the auto sector. A crazy quilt of firms of every shape and size jumped with both feet into America's production offensive. "A metal snow-shovel manufacturer converted his machines to make discs for brakes," one reporter noted at the time. "A vacuum-cleaner maker signed up to turn out specialized aluminum parts. A pesticide squirt-gun maker retooled to crank out hydraulic systems."

Chris-Craft built amphibious vehicles at its works on the St. Clair River northeast of Detroit, as well as its satellites in Cadillac and Holland in west Michigan. These included some of the famous "Higgins Boats" (LCPVs) that would offload soldiers onto the beaches of Anzio, Normandy and islands in the Pacific.

Clayton Lambert produced 40-mm shell casings. Nash-Kelvinator developed the earliest military helicopters, deployed in a limited role in Burma late in the war. And as Detroit Historical Museum curator Joel Stone reminds us, pharmaceutical giant Parke-Davis made penicillin, field dressings and gauze—all crucial to advances in battlefield medicine.

In no time, the padlocks of the Great Depression were a distant memory. The change was evident in the look of things as one moved about the city. One observer put it this way: "This mammoth mass-production machine has a wholly new tempo, a grim new purpose. Busses and trolley cars are jammed. Parking yards around factories and back-alley machine shops are packed with workers' cars. Detroit is busier than it has been for years."

Small enterprises would play a large role in making the $30 billion in war goods (in 1940s dollars) the city would contribute to the fight against the Axis.

But it was the auto concerns that would dominate production. The transition was not without its problems, and industry executives were cautious about committing to military priorities. For one thing, car sales were approaching record highs, a long-awaited return to the black from which it would be hard to walk away under any circumstances. In addition, a bitter taste lingered from the end of the last war, when Washington abruptly canceled contracts and left suppliers high and dry.

"Big Bill" Knudson, Roosevelt's production chief, was uniquely qualified to sell his old colleagues on the "Arsenal of Democracy" program. An immigrant who still spoke with a thick Danish accent, Knudson had risen through the ranks, acquiring along the way a reputation for sound judgment and square dealing. He was admired, too, for his democratic model of management. "Progress is made by average people," Knudson liked to say, thinking of his old co-workers on the line, people whose expertise about the workings of the system came from intimate daily experience.

Pearl Harbor erased any lingering doubts in the auto sector. Detroit's last civilian vehicle rolled off the line in February 1942, and an era of unprecedented cooperation between government and rival car companies was underway.

The array of war goods they made was remarkable. The sprawling Packard Motor Car complex on East Grand was the work of Detroit's master architect Albert Kahn, the son of a German rabbi who contributed so mightily to defeating Hitler's "Thousand-year" *Reich*. Among the specialties at Packard were engines for PT boats and fighter planes. DeSoto, Studebaker and Nash also manufactured aircraft engine parts. Ford's River Rouge facility in Dearborn—another innovative Kahn design, a city in itself with its own steelworks, hospital and 120,000 employees—supplied all manner of vehicles for the armed forces, including the homely but versatile jeep.

Adopting the slogan "Victory is Our Business," General Motors manufactured components for the sleek Avenger fighter plane. Its Oldsmobile division produced artillery shells. Pontiac made 20-mm Oerlikon antiaircraft cannon. Workers at Dodge Main assembled precision gyro-compasses for the navy and mass-produced sturdy ambulances and trucks. Hudson Motors crafted suspension units for tanks. And industry subcontractor National Automotive Fibres switched from making seat covers to an entirely new product line—parachutes.

A similar variety of armaments came out of the auto plants on the south side of the river. The factories of Canada's "Motor City" had a head start on their Detroit counterparts, having been at war since September 1939. And Windsorites were already well familiar with the rationing, air raid drills and anxiety about family members in the field that Americans were just beginning to experience.

Some of the thousands of British children evacuated to Canada during the *Blitz* ended up in Windsor. Host families gave their charges the warmest hospitality, and every effort was made to integrate the youngsters into churches, schools and other neighborhood institutions. But they were still refugees, still homesick, and their plight was poignant testimony to how dire the situation was across the Atlantic.

British refugee children in Windsor. A poignant reminder of the situation across the Atlantic. *Courtesy Reuther Archives.*

Jam Handy was a Detroit-based commercial film company, its portfolio filled with automotive clients. *To New Horizons*, its best-known production, was a short for the GM Pavilion at the New York World's Fair in 1939, dazzling visitors with a car-centric, Jetsons-style model of the far-distant future—in the year 1960. Officials with the Office of War Information understood that its knack for putting complex ideas into vivid, easy-to-understand words and images was a strategic asset, as valuable in its way as the ability to make jeeps or tanks.

At its midtown studios on East Grand, Jam Handy made over seven thousand informational features and training films during the war, tackling subjects as varied as the principles of homefront conservation, the proper way to clean an M-1 rifle and the precautions a soldier should take to avoid contracting a venereal disease. If a young man was in the armed services during World War II, it's a safe bet he saw the creations of Jam Handy.

BIG-NESS

The most potent symbols of the Motor City's prowess were two enormous, purpose-built factories designed by Kahn that would rewrite the books about what was possible in the science of production.

In September 1940, Chrysler broke ground on a one-hundred-acre stretch of farmland in Warren Township due north of Detroit, for a facility to mass-produce M-3 "General Lee" tanks for the military. The site was so remote that construction workers heard pellets hitting their windows as hunters "took aim at quail."

A small railroad was needed to connect operations at the complex, which measured one million square feet in area—five city blocks deep, two blocks wide. Steam from a locomotive provided heat during the first winter until a more permanent power source could be installed. Kahn's blueprint for the structure included safeguards against aerial attack, with three-foot concrete exterior walls and an angled roof to direct bombs away from windows and exhaust fans.

An assortment of army brass, political dignitaries and print and radio journalists—along with line workers, some of them perched atop the roof of the building—were on hand to watch the first M-3 in action. Many thousands more listened to the live radio broadcast. It was a spectacular debut. The tank negotiated mud and craters and smashed a telephone pole to toothpicks without a hitch in its forward momentum.

Under the banner "Enough and On Time," the arsenal would produce the M-3 and, by 1942, the more advanced M-4 "Sherman" in volumes the Axis simply could not match. General Brekon Somerville never doubted

Above: Albert Kahn, Detroit's master architect. *Courtesy Reuther Archives.*

Opposite, top: Teamwork. *Courtesy Warren Historical Society.*

Opposite, bottom: The arsenal's first thirty-ton M-3 tank demonstrates its power, smashing with ease through a telephone pole, April 24, 1941. *Courtesy Warren Historical Society.*

that something this ambitious could be achieved. "When Hitler hitched his chariot to an internal combustion engine," he observed when the Warren works was at full-throttle, "he opened up a new battlefront—a front that we know well. It's called Detroit."

Then there was Henry Ford's bomber factory, perhaps *the* icon of the "can-do" spirit of the war, a production behemoth unparalleled in history. The site chosen for the plant, in Washtenaw County ten miles west of Detroit, near the village of Ypsilanti, was for years a summer camp for boys whose fathers had perished in the Great War. Cultivating soybeans, tapping syrup and tending to apple orchards fed by the Willow Run creek that meandered through its woods and rolling prairie, city kids breathed fresh air and learned the Fordian virtues of work and discipline.

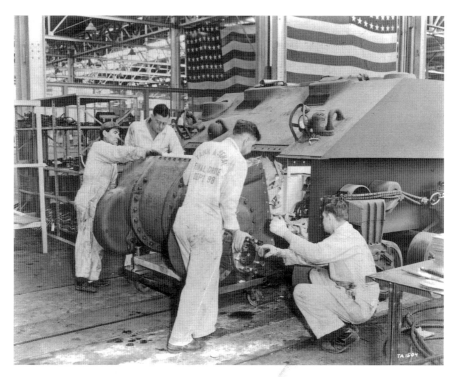

The peace and quiet ended in early 1941, when the Ford Motor Company won a contract to build four-engine B-24 heavy bombers. Before the ink was dry, squadrons of bulldozers were readying the land for a facility equal to the task.

Constructed in only five months at a cost of $100 million, the finished complex spanned two and a half million square feet. Sawing crews were still clearing maple trees as the production machinery was being put into place.

Albert Kahn was famous for bringing light and air into the industrial workplace, but he directed that this three-story structure, his last design, be windowless, as another concession to security. According to automotive historian A.J. Baime, 156,000 forty-watt Sylvania fluorescent bulbs were necessary to illuminate the interior. A one-mile-square airport was carved out adjacent to the site.

Nontechnical considerations dictated Willow Run's curious L shape. Henry Ford insisted on the right angle, no matter the costs or engineering challenges involved, in order to rectify a surveyor's error and keep his works outside of Detroit's Wayne County—in his mind a Sodom of ruinous taxes, bellicose unions and Roosevelt-style Democratic machine politics.

"The Run" featured twin, mile-long assembly lines, the brainchild of no less an authority on mass-production than Charles "Cast Iron" Sorensen, the father of Ford's Model T process a generation earlier. Sorensen remarked later that adapting auto-making techniques to the more stringent performance and safety standards of aircraft was easily the most daunting challenge of his long career.

The idea of applying Detroit's methods to the needs of America's air forces originated from an unlikely source. UAW leader Walter Reuther made headlines in 1940 with his call for "500 Planes a Day" as insurance against threats abroad. Though more a slogan than a plan, Reuther's bold proposal drew attention from the loftiest circles of industry and government, even earning its author an audience with the president in the Oval Office.

The concept was shelved, again mostly for political reasons. The thought of a union man so brazenly attempting to influence industrial policy made auto insiders uneasy, to say the least, and executives at Douglass, Lockheed and Boeing did not welcome an incursion of amateurs onto their turf. Resistance faded, though, as the world situation deteriorated. Now, at Willow Run, the dream of mass-producing large combat aircraft was about to be put to the test.

The cantankerous Mr. Ford, by this time in his late seventies, was in on the broad outlines of the project, imposing his views about the shape of the building and insisting that the works include both manufacturing and assembly operations. But it was Sorensen and Henry's son Edsel—in Maury Klein's judgment, "the twin pillars of sanity at Ford"—who were charged with its execution, and it was they would receive credit or blame for its performance.

The younger Ford had a flexibility of mind and human touch his father so notoriously lacked. It was Edsel who in 1941 persuaded his father to bow to the inevitable and accept collective bargaining with his workers. (An ultimatum on the issue from Henry's wife, Clara, also helped to bring the old man along.) It was Edsel, too, who convinced Mr. Ford to swallow his isolationist sentiments and take up the challenge of war production.

The pressure on Edsel Ford was intense, and the price he ultimately paid was a high one. He worked late into the night overseeing all aspects of the plant's start-up phase, in spite of severe stomach pains that would prove to be symptoms of terminal cancer, claiming his life in 1943. "The war won't wait," he told the doctors who ordered him to slow down.

Edsel gave Sorensen free rein in devising an alternative to what they had seen on a tour of West Coast aircraft plants. Managers at a San Diego facility seemed content to fabricate one or two handcrafted "Liberators" per day. Without consulting his son or his chief engineer, Henry Ford summoned the press and announced that *his* system, once up and running, would spit planes out at the rate of one per *hour*—around the clock, seven days a week.

Ford's bravado certainly pushed Willow Run into the center of the national spotlight. The audacity of its ambition was irresistible to a country still shaken in its confidence and aching to deliver retribution. In the popular imagination, the idea of Willow Run fit perfectly with the civic faith in technology, limitless frontiers and *big-ness*. "It is a promise of revenge for Pearl Harbor," the *Detroit Free Press* bluntly asserted. In time "the Lib" would take its place alongside the jeep, the M-1 rifle, the Flying Fortress and the Norden bombsight as an expression of American ingenuity and righteous might.

The scrutiny grew even more intense when Charles Lindbergh arrived to assume duties as a trouble-shooting consultant on the project.

Lindbergh and Mr. Ford had been friends and mutual admirers for some time. The Lone Eagle stayed at the auto baron's Fair Lane estate in Dearborn during trips to the area to see his mother. Despite their differences in age, the two men had much in common, both good and bad. Both were, at heart, reclusive farm boys more comfortable in the presence of machinery than people. Both were lionized as models of rugged individualism. And both attracted criticism for accepting medals from *Herr* Hitler's regime and making crudely anti-Semitic public statements. Because of his lobbying with America First, Colonel Lindbergh was *persona non grata* in the eyes of the Roosevelt administration, and efforts to reactivate his old army commission after Pearl Harbor were denied. Taking the job with Ford was a way for this restless man to contribute his talents to the war effort while still maintaining his independence and freedom of movement.

Lindbergh was awestruck when he first entered Willow Run's main building, declaring what he saw "a sort of Grand Canyon of the mechanized world." The high-altitude test flights he performed during his months at the project proved to be of great value, and needless to say, his design suggestions received a warm welcome from company engineers.

Progress toward Mr. Ford's Olympian goal was, however, painfully slow. It took longer than expected to train line workers, and the modifications continually demanded by air corps officials brought things repeatedly to a standstill. The snail's pace was an embarrassment when Missouri senator Harry Truman came to town for a look with his subcommittee on defense waste and fraud in the spring of 1942.

Six months later, the news was not much better. The Arsenal of Democracy's ballyhooed cathedral of production had managed by then to turn out only one B-24, on September 10. Morale sagged, and rates of absenteeism and employee turnover were running intolerably high. In one month during this period, Ford hired 2,900 workers—only to lose 3,100. Detractors, led by spokesmen from the aircraft industry, delighted in asking the question, "Willit Run?"

"Too often America's mobilization has been portrayed as a smoothly flowing process," Maury Klein has written. More often the opposite was true. The ramping up of munitions work in Detroit and elsewhere was a complicated, uneven process plagued by shortages, mistakes and poor planning. Getting all the moving pieces to work together was "an arduous, chaotic, contentious grind that exacted a high physical and psychic toll" on everyone involved, as the tragic case of Edsel Ford illustrates. Remembering this reality, rather than the airbrushed myth, makes the production achievements of World War II all the more astonishing.

"A GOOD DRIVE!"

A week later, the president and Mrs. Roosevelt embarked on a two-week inspection tour of war plants and military installations around the country. To limit disruptions, FDR directed that the itinerary be secret, "off the record" as far as reporters were concerned. And officials at each facility were to be given as little advance notice as possible, often as late as the day of the visit.

The first stop was, appropriately, Detroit. From the start of the day on September 18, 1942, the beaming, hat-waving chief executive was in full campaign mode, acknowledging with relish the "thunderous" cheers that erupted the minute he appeared on the train platform of the Chrysler Tank Arsenal. As the famous "Sunshine Special" Lincoln convertible moved forward slowly through the plant, lucky workers got close enough to share a word with the president and shake his hand. The First Lady was all smiles that afternoon, too, gratified to see so many women on the job. Their contributions would be the subject of her next "My Day" syndicated column.

The VIPs got a close-up view of the gear-cutting process and then watched as transmissions and engines were lowered onto tank chassis. Next, the proceedings moved outdoors to the arsenal's figure-eight test track, for a chance to observe the speed and maneuverability of the new M-4 tank.

There was a tense moment when one of the Shermans, "making a terrific din and throwing up a whirlwind of mud and dust," came barreling directly toward the president's car, pulling up just short ("not many feet") of

Above: "A good drive!" Observing the new M-4 Sherman up close. *Courtesy FDR Library.*

Opposite, top: Surprise visitor. President Roosevelt on the train platform of the Warren Tank Arsenal, September 18, 1942. *Courtesy FDR Library.*

Opposite, bottom: The president and Mrs. Roosevelt listen attentively as Chrysler CEO Kenneth Keller explains the tank assembly process. *Courtesy FDR Library.*

catastrophe. Secret Service agents were not amused by this demonstration of the vehicle's braking system, but the man they protected seemed unruffled, putting everyone at ease with his trademark wry humor. "A good drive!" he announced to the crew, tossing his head back with a hearty laugh.

Now the scene shifted west to Willow Run. Lindbergh had gotten wind of the impending festivities and absented himself for the day. Henry Ford, another Roosevelt adversary, came to wish he had called in sick too. A hastily assembled search detail located him lying low in a remote corner of the plant, and it took some firm persuasion to get him to force a smile and climb into the back seat with the guests.

One has to appreciate the comic aspects of the ride that followed. Edsel and Sorensen were in jump seats across from Mr. Ford, and the meaning of his stony silence was not lost on them. "Sitting between the Roosevelts, who were good-sized people, he was almost hidden," Sorensen recalled later. "He could not enter into the spirit of the event. When Edsel or I turned to look at him he would glare at us furiously."

The host's torment simmered as his employees—men and women, white, black and brown, union members all—abandoned their work stations to whistle and clap while the limousine inched along. Edsel and Sorensen explained each step in the production process, the president and First Lady asked many questions and the event went well beyond its scheduled time.

As America moved into its second full year of war, the momentum was shifting in favor of the Allies, thanks in large part to the blizzard of tanks, planes and ordnance pouring out of Detroit and other industrial centers. The enemy was tenacious, there were much blood yet to be spilled and the bottlenecks and breakdowns that plagued the munitions plants would never be completely eliminated. But the big picture was definitely brightening. "This is the record," administration spokesman Donald

Henry Ford, right, manages a smile as the president works the crowd at Willow Run. *Courtesy FDR Library.*

Nelson declared during a Washington speech. "For nine years before Pearl Harbor, Germany, Italy and Japan prepared intensively for war, while as late as 1940 the war production of peaceful America was virtually nothing. Yet two years later the output of our war factories is equal to that of the three Axis nations combined."

With a bit of hyperbole, a reporter covering the industrial scene calculated that the combined output of domestic arms makers was "the equivalent of building two Panama Canals every day."

In his 1943 State of the Union, President Roosevelt was able to report "miraculous" production numbers, exceeding in many categories the targets he had outlined the year before. "These facts and figures will give no great aid and comfort to the enemy," he added with undisguised satisfaction. "I suspect that Hitler and Tojo will find it difficult to explain to the German and Japanese people just why it is that 'decadent, inefficient democracy' can produce such phenomenal quantities of munitions—and fighting men."

The Run more than made up for its slow start, rolling out a new bomber every sixty-three minutes by the end of 1943. Henry Ford was a hero again, linked in the public mind with Henry Kaiser, the man who could build a "Liberty Ship" in only fourteen days.

Ford's operations, extending to the horizon, overwhelmed the senses. "It is impossible in words to convey the feel and smell and tension of Willow Run under full headway," one worker marveled. It demanded a kind of poetry: "The roar of the machinery, the special din of the riveting gun absolutely deafening nearby, the throbbing crash of the giant metal presses, the far-reaching line of half-born skyships growing wings under swarms of workers, and the restless cranes swooping overhead."

The aircraft Willow Run produced had considerable impact on the war's changing fortunes. Notable for its range and durability, the B-24 was a workhorse for the army air corps in campaigns from North Africa and western Europe to Burma and Japan. Its signature moment was an assault on Hitler's oil refineries near Ploesti, Romania, on August 1, 1943. The mission was no milk run—many planes and many lives were lost—but it dealt a powerful blow to the fuel supplies of the Third Reich.

A healthy spirit of competition and teamwork drove munitions workers beyond what might have been considered their limits in peacetime. Chrysler's Tank Arsenal was the first facility to receive the Army-Navy Production Excellence Award, an honor reserved for plants that met or exceeded quotas while delivering the highest quality. Banners were unveiled with great fanfare

"The far-reaching line of half-born sky ships growing wings." The B-24 plant at full capacity. *Courtesy Yankee Air Museum.*

at each facility as managers and employees stood side by side to watch, sporting their new "E" pins with justifiable pride.

The speaker at the Willow Run ceremony in May 1944 was Henry Ford II, released from his duties as a naval officer in the Pacific to manage operations after his father's untimely death. Henry II called the award a tribute to the vision of Edsel Ford and "just another proof that in America we can do the impossible."

ROSIE AND FRIENDS
GO TO WAR

As America mobilized for war, the workforce in Detroit's factories swelled with unprecedented speed. At its peak, Willow Run alone had forty-two thousand employees. With the tight labor market, many of the newly hired were African Americans, Hispanics and other minorities, eager to seize opportunities for good-paying jobs denied them in peacetime.

Companies dropped old eligibility restrictions, written and unwritten, and actively recruited people once considered too old or infirm for the rigors of factory work. State governments relaxed child labor laws, and disabled people were welcomed into plants to perform tasks appropriate to their skills. Recruited from circus troupes and Hollywood back lots, ten "midgets" (to use the term of the day) roamed the grounds of The Run, conducting inspections and "bucking" rivets inside the tight spaces of the Lib's fuselage and wing sections.

Regulations barring discrimination by defense contractors certainly accelerated the changes, but they would have come to some degree in any case. Under the circumstances, common sense trumped prejudice and stereotype, and turning away qualified applicants was a luxury the country simply could not afford.

Women—the "Rosie the Riveters" of World War II mythology—proved their mettle in all kinds of jobs in the wartime defense industry. Because of their presumed dexterity, they were at first limited to precision tasks: assembling engine wiring harnesses for tanks, sewing parachutes, upholstering aircraft seats, installing grenade fuses, molding plexiglass nose cones and filling metal casings with gunpowder.

But soon they were doing heavier labor—operating jigs, lathes, drill and punch-presses, grinding and milling machines; soldering and arc welding; and maneuvering giant cranes and forklifts. Some worked uniformed security details, sidearms at the ready as they patrolled the factory perimeter.

In most cases, women worked apart from the men and were compensated less for their efforts. But it was still much more than they could expect to make in traditionally "female" occupations. "I couldn't wait to get up here and get in the bomber plant," remembered one Rosie. "In Kentucky as a hotel waitress I made only $2.40 a day. Here, I could make $10.85." In many plants, women constituted a third or more of the workforce.

Used to eking out a living as nannies, cooks and maids, black women were especially glad to find the factory doors open during the war. They were assigned noisier, dirtier and more dangerous jobs than their lighter-skinned sisters, many of whom expressed unease at the thought of working beside them. They shouldered back-straining loads, they sprayed

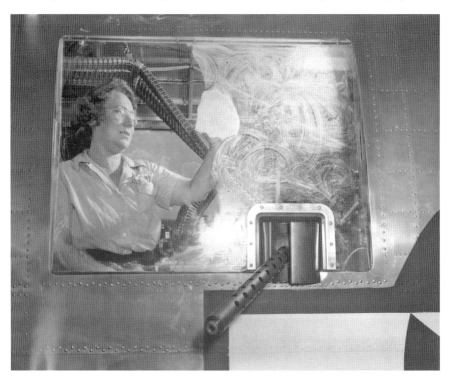

Finishing work on a Liberator cockpit. *Courtesy Yankee Air Museum.*

"Rosie the Riveter" at The Run. *Courtesy Yankee Air Museum.*

toxic paints and dyes and a few toiled in the inferno of the foundries. But for most, the rewards, including the chance to be part of a team doing meaningful work, made the hardships bearable. A black Rosie caught the irony of the situation: "Hitler was the one that got us out of the white folks' kitchen."

The newcomers were not universally welcomed, however, and hazing and harassment on the shop floor were all too common, especially in the early stages of the wartime "experiment." One woman recalled the loneliness of her first day:

> *It was a big room with a high ceiling and fluorescent lights, and it was very noisy. I walked in there in my overalls, and suddenly all the machines stopped and every guy in the shop just turned around and looked at me. It took, I think, two weeks before anyone even talked to me. The discrimination was indescribable. They wanted to kill me. My attitude was…I'm going to prove to you I can do anything you can do, and maybe better than some of you. And that's exactly the way it turned out.*

Managers (almost always men) were called on to adapt the workplace to the demands of going coed. They had to resolve issues ranging from the allocation of washrooms (and, in the more progressive shops, child-care facilities) to cleaning up the speech and demeanor of their shop foremen. "Watch Your Language There Are Women Present," read signs posted in break areas and other shared spaces.

With toughness and skill, the workingwomen of World War II won at least the grudging respect of their male counterparts. They were valued for brains as well as brawn, too, encouraged to keep their fresh eyes open for ways to do things more efficiently. During a visit to Detroit's Packard complex, Eleanor Roosevelt presented a leadership award to Bernice Palmer, a line worker responsible for suggesting more production shortcuts than any other employee in the plant.

"I had a time convincing my husband to let me go," Betty Oelke recalled of her journey to Willow Run in 1942. And it was not just a matter of physical distance. Armed with her new husband's blessing, Betty went out and purchased her first-ever pair of trousers and then delivered herself to the employment office of the great bomber plant. She started with a five-day workweek, but it went to six as production kicked into overdrive.

Betty's shifts involved exacting, physically demanding labor. After punching the clock, she was on her feet for nine hours at a stretch, minus a few short breaks, drilling holes in one aluminum panel after another to prep it for the rivets another woman would insert down the line. Each B-24 required over 300,000 rivets, and just *one* improperly installed compromised the entire plane. Removing and replacing it would have a ripple effect, slowing everything down, so the women responsible got very good at avoiding such mistakes.

Betty and her coworkers felt the constant, unforgiving eyes of their supervisors on them as they tended to their business. "They would stand right there and time you. We were expected to keep up. If you didn't, you were reprimanded." For all its pressures, though, Betty loved her job. She earned a bonus for returning to work only three weeks after the birth of her first child, and she maintained an otherwise perfect attendance record throughout the war.

Willow Run employee Rose Will Monroe was one of several women to inspire the "Rosie the Riveter" icon so widely remembered today. Another was Inkster-born Geraldine Hoff Doyle, a metal press operator in Ann Arbor who posed for the "We Can Do It!" poster designed by J. Howard Miller for Westinghouse. Together they projected a swagger not previously associated with the "fairer sex."

As one of nine children growing up in the coal country of Pulaski County, Kentucky, Monroe had to scratch for everything just to survive. When the war plants started hiring, she realized that her knack for fixing machinery was a ticket to a better life up north. Picked out of a crowd to appear in an OWI film about teamwork on the homefront, Monroe personified the qualities celebrated in Kay Kyser's jukebox anthem of the day, co-written by Redd Evans and John Jacob Loeb:

All the day long whether rain or shine
　　She's a part of the assembly line
She's making history
　　working for victory.
While other girls attend a favorite
　　cocktail bar,
Sipping dry martinis,
　　munching caviar;
There's a girl who's putting them
　　to shame—
Rosie the Riveter is her name.
Keeps a sharp lookout for sabotage
　　Sitting up there on the fuselage
That little frail can do
　　more than a male will do
ROSIE THE RIVETER!

Millions of women fit this description, more or less—each a real-life "Rosie" (or a "Wendy the Welder") doing her bit, and then some, for her country.

There were proposals in Washington to conscript women for munitions work, but these faded as it became clear that appeals for voluntary service would be more than sufficient to meet the demand. The U.S. Employment Service targeted its recruitment campaigns to places where the need was most acute. In the Motor City, 600,000 households received registration cards in the mail asking the women of the family to list their education and employment history. The data helped in matching respondents to compatible jobs.

Magazine ads reassured housewives they would be able to navigate the transition from home to factory without difficulty. In her study *Rosie the Riveter Revisited*, Sherna Berger Gluck summed up the message: "If you could operate a sewing machine, you could easily learn to run a drill or a punch press or a rivet gun." Ford's widely distributed promotional film *Women on the Warpath* drove home the same point.

Young women out of high school were deluged with appeals to their patriotism and, to a degree, their sense of guilt. With brothers and boyfriends putting their lives on the line far from home, the least a girl could do was help out in a war plant. "Do the Job He Left Behind," urged one OWI poster. "The More WOMEN at Work, the SOONER we Win!" declared another. Even those in office and clerical fields were cast as part of a united front against the Axis. A roadside billboard featured a secretary full of determination looking up from her typewriter. "Victory Waits on YOUR Fingers—Keep 'em Flying, Miss U.S.A."

Vanity was another factor taken into account in recruitment offensives, reflecting the stereotypes of the day. A lady need not surrender her softer side when she put on dungarees and got her hands dirty. "Magazines demonstrated how war workers could be glamorous, even fashionable," Gluck writes. Plants sometimes sponsored Victory Fashion Shows during the lunch hour, with employees modeling the latest in work and leisure-time apparel. In 1942, there was a nationwide competition for "Miss Victory," but the emphasis was on her work ethic rather than how she filled out a bathing suit. "I've never been tardy or absent," a finalist proudly told the judges during her screening interview. Gluck describes for us the fast-changing cultural landscape:

> *Movies portrayed the likes of Ginger Rogers dressed in slacks with a snood on her head tooling around the aircraft plant on a forklift. Norman Rockwell memorialized the young war worker on the cover of the* Saturday

Evening Post—*a muscular but pert, rosy-cheeked young woman, rivet gun slung across her lap. [H]er loafer-clad foot was firmly planted on* Mein Kampf—*symbolizing her role in stamping out fascism—but she could remain feminine, as the powder puff and mirror peeking out of her coverall reminded.*

Rockwell's illustration was, in a real sense, divinely inspired. The model for the stout figure with lipstick, rouge and polished nails was Mary Keefe, a neighbor from his small town in Vermont, but he borrowed the regal pose, halo adorning a bandana-clad head, from Michelangelo's Sistine Chapel fresco of the prophet Isaiah.

The oral history archive at Willow Run's Yankee Air Museum preserves the experiences of many of the men and women who worked there during the war years. Their richly individual stories don't need the embellishments of slick posters or glossy magazines to be of interest to us today.

One Rosie recalled how eager she was, like Betty Oelke, to leave her sleepy Michigan hamlet to work on the B-24. Assigned to a team assembling cockpit floors, after six months she was handed a clipboard and moved up to a supervisory position in Quality Assurance.

When a floor passed her inspection, she stamped it with a metal die bearing her initials. For her, the ritual was personal, sealing the bond of trust she felt with the crews who would fly the planes in the line of fire. "We couldn't fight overseas," she explained, "but we all had brothers, sons, husbands and fathers fighting for us. I would not have been doing my part to help those men if I did not make sure that all those parts were perfect."

"BOMBER CITY?"

The influx of war workers and their families into Detroit brought with it a host of logistical and social challenges. The most pressing, and potentially the most explosive, was the question of housing. Not many new dwellings had been built during the Depression decade, and much of what was now available was substandard, dilapidated and in any case already occupied to the limit.

Newcomers placed ads and turned to word-of-mouth networks to avoid price gouging by landlords and find rents they could afford. For obvious reasons, single men had an easier time of it than heads of families. Boardinghouse residents worked schedules out among themselves for day and night shifts in the same lumpy cot, sofa or Murphy bed—"hot bunks," they were called. To keep the noise down during the day, they posted "War Workers Sleeping" signs outside their cramped quarters.

The housing situation was especially dire for whites recruited from Kentucky, Tennessee and Alabama, many of whom had arrived in town with only what they could cram into a cloth satchel or a cardboard suitcase. To discourage such "undesirables," vacancy notices often specified "No Southerners."

The choices available to African Americans were even more limited. "Colored" families were confined to a few overcrowded enclaves in the city, most famously the "Black Bottom" district just east of downtown. Squatters filled the parks and set up makeshift dwellings in empty buildings, attracting unwanted attention from the police.

Willow Run had its own housing crisis. In view of the sixty-mile commute to and from the city, employees naturally wanted to live close to work, but plans to accommodate them ranged from inadequate to nonexistent. Servicemen, too, were affected by the disarray. Pilots waiting to fly B-24s off the line to airfields across the country struggled to catch sleep amid the rows of cots set up for them in one of The Run's drafty, cavernous hangars.

One answer to the problem under consideration was an ambitious, federally funded community for thirty thousand, to be called Bomber City. Noted modernist architect Oskar Stonorov was commissioned to create a blueprint, and even FDR backed the idea in its general outlines. The plan was scaled back and then scuttled, however, in the face of fierce local opposition.

To Henry Ford, Bomber City was a boondoggle, pure and simple, one more New Deal–style intrusion into his private affairs and a waste of strategic materials to boot. Under cover of night, company agents pulled up surveyor stakes to make sure the message got across. And in a series of town hall meetings, residents of Ypsilanti expressed their horror at the prospect of a permanent "slum" in their backyard once the demand for unskilled labor leveled off.

This two-family duplex was typical of the dwellings available to Willow Run employees and their families. *Courtesy Yankee Air Museum.*

Cramped quarters. *Courtesy Yankee Air Museum.*

Ford built a few modest dormitories for his employees, but most were left to find their own solutions. Workers and their families moved into encampments of tents, trailers and tar-paper shacks that look in photographs like the Hoovervilles of the Great Depression. Access to heat and water in these communities was uncertain at best, and the ground under one's feet froze in winter and turned to quicksand with the spring rains. Schooling for the children was sporadic and of questionable quality.

Still, people made homes of their ramshackle dwellings, helping one another with day-to-day challenges and counting the blessings of a steady paycheck.

Getting to and from the job was another issue. Some lived close enough to walk: the Willow Run "campers," the Highland Park employees who clocked in at the Ford complex a few blocks from their rented rooms and the Hamtramck men and women who pulled long shifts at Dodge Main.

For greater distances, there was a dense web of buses and streetcars, a transit system that would surprise residents of today's Motor City with its efficiency and reach. Bells clanging, electric streetcars rolled up and down the spokes of Detroit's original city plan—one per minute at peak times. Routes on Michigan Avenue, Grand River, Woodward, Gratiot and Jefferson anchored a network spanning more than five hundred miles. At times, the cars were packed to bursting with factory workers, soldiers and mothers with their cranky, restless children in tow. But a nickel fare, with transfers, put the sprawling city at your feet.

As in the defense plants, a labor shortage opened doors to applicants once excluded from high-wage transit and service jobs. People got used to seeing uniformed women pumping gas and under the hood checking the oil, and their presence aboard sanitation and street-cleaning trucks was so ordinary after a while that it drew no notice. "Motorettes" were behind the wheel in taxis, and "conductorettes" sat in the front of buses and streetcars.

When the City of Detroit began hiring African Americans for these positions—in token numbers at first—it was evident that not everyone approved. James Jenkins started on the buses in 1941 and could recall decades later the open hostility he and his fellow black drivers routinely

Streetcar scene in downtown Detroit. One stop on a network spanning over five hundred miles. *Courtesy Reuther Archives.*

Off-duty. Mrs. Marguerite Watson, Detroit's first "conductorette." *Courtesy Reuther Archives.*

encountered on the job. Some whites simply refused to ride with them. "We used to laugh about it," Jenkins explained with a smile. "We used to pull up in front of the Fisher Building on the Dexter bus going to Fullerton or Fenkell and open the doors, and they'd turn their back on you. Me and a guy would holler out, 'Well, you better come on and ride with me. The one behind me is blacker than I am!'"

Humor was one way to cope with the indignities of Jim Crow. But the depth and sheer pettiness of the racism of those days is hard for us to fathom now. "People used to get on and we had to make change," Jenkins remembered, shaking his head. "They used to take their money and hold it in a way that they didn't have to touch your hand."

Driving was a commuting alternative—*if* you had a car, a set of serviceable tires (usually patched and paper-thin) and access to that most precious of wartime commodities, gasoline. Carpooling was the rule, with riders sharing maintenance and repair expenses for a vehicle often years past its prime. The more daring took to Detroit's sleek new superhighways, built to connect the war plants but open, also, to public use. Barbara Williams recalled that just the word "expressway" had a mesmerizing effect on her teenage imagination. Expecting some kind of magic carpet ride, she was disappointed to find out it was "just another road" when her father took the family out on one for a trial run.

Completed early in the war, the Davison, "the world's first urban depressed freeway," serviced the factories of Highland Park and Hamtramck. The east–west Edsel Ford Expressway—today's I-94—carried traffic between Willow Run and the Rouge. And the north–south Chrysler freeway, today's I-75, connected the Warren Tank Arsenal to suppliers and rail facilities downtown near the Detroit River.

Unprecedented in scale and expense, these public works projects had an impact that went far beyond their immediate purposes. After the war, they would serve as arteries speeding the flight of people and jobs out to the suburbs.

A UNION LABEL
IN BERLIN

As we have seen, munitions work was a patriotic endeavor during World War II, and those engaged in it felt a special responsibility to the soldiers, sailors and airmen who were fighting in their name. Washington made every effort to keep civilians aware of their homefront duties.

The first and most important of these was to keep the production lines moving. An OWI poster admonished citizens that "Too Little, Too Late—Is Out of Date!" An ad in the pro-labor *Free Press*, meanwhile, warned its rank-and-file readership that this was not the time to press trivial grievances. "[S]trikes, sit-downs and work stoppages of any kind only hurt Old Glory and help Hitler."

Another Norman Rockwell illustration showed a GI dug in and under fire as the ammo on his machine gun belt ran perilously low. The look of desperation said it all. "LET'S GIVE HIM ENOUGH AND ON TIME," read the caption. A sign displayed in many factories took a different tack, with a grinning Japanese viper urging Americans to "Go Ahead, Please—TAKE THE DAY OFF!" And this popular slogan delivered the message with maximum economy: "The Guy Who Relaxes Is Helping the Axis."

Detroit was a center of organizing activity in the 1930s, often accompanied by violent confrontations between labor and management. By the time of Pearl Harbor, most autoworkers were dues-paying members of the UAW, and Walter Reuther and others in the leadership did their best to head off conflicts, announcing a "no strike" pledge for the duration. There *were* breaches—unauthorized "wildcat" strikes, some venting rage at the hiring and promotion of blacks, Hispanics and women. But these were isolated and usually of short duration.

Employees who refused to join a hate strike did so out of a mixture of common sense and conscience. Ernie Zipser, an American-born son of Hungarian Jews (and a proud UAW member), remained at his work station in the Hudson Plant when a protest over the hiring of a "colored" employee erupted one afternoon. "I wasn't about to leave that S.O.B. [his drill press]," Zipser explained, with a flash of anger. "I couldn't believe that we were fighting a war for democracy and the rights of people, and when a black man gets on the machine, everybody walks out. What kind of sh-t is that? It's hypocrisy."

The sleeping giant awakened. *Courtesy Office of War Information.*

But stoppages over more legitimate issues were considered one more front in the global struggle for human dignity. "My brother is in Italy," a woman picketing in support of the United Rubber Workers told a reporter in early 1945. "He wrote me before we went on strike to fight for our rights over here. That's what we're doing." Some union figures were granted deferments in recognition of their role in maintaining labor peace, including young, pugnacious Jimmy Hoffa, a rising star in the Teamsters.

Men and women adorned the tanks, planes and jeeps they built with crucifixes and Stars of David, as well as graffiti predicting the early demise of Hitler and Tojo. (The men in the field later added their *own* artwork, usually in the form of scantily clad pin-up models.) They embedded notes of blessing and good luck into the seams and crevices of the war machines, addressed to the men whose lives depended on their reliability and performance. Officially against the rules, they were poignant human touches to which supervisors almost always turned a blind eye.

Wartime employees at Detroit's auto plants took satisfaction from the fact that the *imprimatur* of their brotherhood was embossed on their creations. A raucous drinking song of the day expressed the feeling:

> *There'll be a union-label in Berlin*
> *when the union boys in uniform*
> *march in!*
>
> *And rolling in the ranks there'll be*
> *UAW tanks—*
> *Roll Hitler out*
> *and roll the union in!*

PART II
THE MILITARY MOTOR CITY

MESSAGE FROM THE PAST

On a warm July day in 2014, David Losinski took his son Drew scuba diving in Lake Huron, northeast of Detroit. As volunteers for the Michigan Department of Environmental Quality, they were there collecting water samples in an area where a commercial barge had recently gone down.

In the depths, the pair noticed a tangle of metal, mysterious but something obviously manmade. When they returned for a closer look, its identity was apparent. "Dad, that's an airplane!" young Drew exclaimed when they came up to the surface.

What these amateur marine archaeologists had chanced upon were the remains of a P-39 Aircobra fighter from World War II—engine, wings, fuselage and tail section. A serial number made it possible to trace it to the crash that killed its pilot, Frank Moody of Los Angeles, some seventy years earlier, on April 11, 1944.

Moody was a member of the 332nd Fighter Group of the famed Tuskegee Airmen, the black fliers who trained for a time at nearby Selfridge Field. He perished during a test flight that revealed flaws in the design of the aircraft, and because of what he did, others would be spared a similar fate.

The Lake Huron discovery is a message from the past, about heroism and sacrifice and about our connection to the struggle Lieutenant Moody and millions like him once waged on our behalf. The site is now protected and will remain undisturbed, as a place to reflect on the debts we owe to this extraordinary generation of Americans.

"DIM THOSE LIGHTS!"

Frank Moody's plane returns us to a time when Detroit was mobilized for war, and indeed, the city took on the features of a garrison after Pearl Harbor. Within hours of the first bulletins from Hawaii, soldiers were dispatched to guard locations throughout the world's most important industrial center.

Airfields went on maximum alert. Freighters plying the busy Detroit River were subject to heightened levels of inspection. State troopers were visible at the white-marbled Livingstone Memorial Lighthouse on the east end of Belle Isle, facing out to Lake St. Clair. Spotters with logbooks synchronized watches to War Time, an energy-saving measure equivalent to today's Daylight Savings Time. Searchlights probed the night skies, looking for any sign of danger.

Sandbags appeared around Detroit's power plants and communication centers, and humorless sentries with bayonets fixed turned away all but the most essential visitors. Machine gun mounts were installed on the roof of WWJ Radio's headquarters on Eight Mile Road and the Fisher Building in the New Center, home to WJR, the fifty-thousand-watt "Great Voice of the Great Lakes."

Transport links were placed under twenty-four-hour surveillance. Notable among these was Belle Isle's Douglas MacArthur Bridge, so renamed early in 1942 to honor the hero of the Pacific Theater, whose famous vow to return as he evacuated the Philippines bolstered spirits besieged by bad news. From Bataan and Corregidor to the rough seas of the North Atlantic, where

Beefing up security on the border with Canada. *Courtesy Reuther Archives.*

U-boat wolf packs preyed at will on supply convoys to Britain, it was obvious to all that things were not going well. Edginess caused by these reversals surely accounts for the record attendance churches everywhere experienced on Easter Sunday that spring.

Public service announcements cautioned people to use discretion in talking about their jobs or the contents of letters from their boys in uniform. Civilians were told to be on the alert for spies and enemy agents, especially around the big munitions plants. "No Room for Rumors," read one poster circulated by the Office of War Information. "The Saboteur's Greatest Weapon Is Arson," declared another.

BE VIGILANT
BE ALERT
BE CAREFUL

Never forget that America's Front Line Is the Production Line!

After the 1941 Christmas season, a lot of lights and other downtown decorations were put away for the duration. How *long* the new, monochromatic austerity would last—and *when* (if ever) "normalcy" might return—was anybody's guess. But a hard road lay ahead, even under the most optimistic scenarios.

Street-level windows at Detroit's prestige department stores—J.L. Hudson's, Crowley's and Kern's—were enlisted to promote the war effort, as were those of the more budget-friendly Kresge's, Woolworth's and Sam's. The public needed to be educated about what was at stake, and these spaces were perfect for the job. Whimsical themes gave way to flag-draped portraits of Roosevelt and MacArthur, appeals for blood donations and war bond sales and reproductions of the Constitution. Sometimes they displayed captured weapons or uniforms bearing swastikas and rising suns.

In September 1942, Hudson's sponsored the Detroit stop of the "Four Freedoms" show, a lavish traveling exhibition celebrating the high principles for which the country was fighting, as outlined by the president: freedom of speech and worship and freedom from want and fear. Nearly 300,000 lined

A window at J.L. Hudson's department store downtown. *Courtesy Detroit Historical Society.*

the parade route along Woodward to watch. The store used the occasion to unfurl its multistory Old Glory, "World's Largest Flag," resplendent with its forty-eight stars.

Ostentatious behavior was out of favor during World War II, condemned as selfish, wasteful and just plain bad taste. The pursuit of personal gain, luxury and comfort had to wait until the storm passed. Blackouts and "dim-outs" caused inconveniences for everyone, but most people took them in stride. The need to "go dark" was as unavoidable as the weather, so why complain? Besides, the black curtains used to contain light in your neighborhood were identical to the ones installed in the White House and the Capitol building in Washington. Nobody, regardless of station, was exempt from the rules.

And make no mistake about it, the threat seemed real and imminent. "Enemy ships could swoop in and shell New York," FDR remarked during an impromptu press conference in February 1942. "Enemy planes could drop bombs on war plants in Detroit. Enemy troops could attack Alaska." An OWI poster pulled no punches about the gravity of the danger, depicting a toddler in tears over his dead mother, surrounded by rubble after an air raid. Whether the image was from Liverpool, Warsaw or Nanking was less important than its shock value:

> MURDER *in Detroit…*
>
> *It* CAN *Happen Here!*
>
> *Think Detroiters! And think before it's too late. Is this to be* your *loved ones lying broken in the ruins of your home? Is this* your *child, motherless or maimed?*
>
> *If you're one of those who said we'd whip the Japs in two weeks, better think again. You and your loved ones here in Detroit and all that you hold dear are definitely "military objectives" on Hitler's and Hirohito's dive-bombing schedule. And why not? For Detroit is turning out more of the things Hitler fears than any other city on earth.*

Messages like this one brought the distant war home very effectively.

The Office of Strategic Services solicited maps and vacation photos of Europe and Asia from the public, casting a wide net in search of anything that might help Allied soldiers negotiate the terrain they would have to cross with hot steel flying. The campaign yielded intelligence that saved many lives.

More than 100,000 Detroiters volunteered to serve as air wardens and auxiliary firefighters during the war. Civil defense was, by its nature, a

Detroit schoolchildren in a civil defense drill. *Courtesy Reuther Archives.*

loose and often chaotic affair, with practices varying significantly from one neighborhood council to another. This was a small price to pay, though, for an appropriately democratic response to the nation's security needs, one that invited citizens to participate in their own defense in a spirit of teamwork and mutual aid.

The runaway bestseller in bookshops in 1942 was not a romance novel or detective story, but the *Red Cross First Aid Handbook*, required reading for wardens everywhere. Identifiable by their white helmets, armbands and no-nonsense demeanor, "Dim those lights!" was their battle cry as they policed "leakages" and made sure car headlights were set on low-beam and half-taped or painted over (giving them the appearance of hooded eyelids).

Wardens gave an earful and sometimes a ticket to those who were in any way careless about public safety. They gave workshops at schools and libraries and urged every family to keep food, water and blackout candles on hand in the event of an emergency. It was also a good idea to designate a "refuge room" at the center of one's dwelling. Civil defense officials in Detroit were issued gas masks, manufactured locally at the Eureka Vacuum Cleaner Company. Since there weren't enough to go around, how they would be distributed during an alert—a potentially life-and-death decision—was left entirely to their judgment.

National Civil Defense chief Fiorello LaGuardia, the colorful and streetwise mayor of New York, set the tone for wartime public safety in language anyone could understand. "Don't be a wise guy and get killed. Be prudent and *live*." Detroit's volunteers did their jobs conscientiously, keeping vigil for attacks that, fortunately, never came.

WARRIORS IN OUR MIDST

In the Military Motor City, it was normal to see men and women in uniform out and about—patronizing stores and theaters, sitting at drugstore counters and walking in twos and threes amid the sidewalk crowds downtown. Olive drab and khaki were the colors for 1942. On buses and streetcars, a civilian was expected to give up his seat to a soldier, and a sergeant's stripes or a pair of navy wings practically guaranteed the bearer a lift in a car, a spot at the front of the line in a restaurant, a free (or at least heavily discounted) pass to a Tigers game and all the drinks they could handle at the local watering hole. People demonstrated appreciation for their service in many ways. Hanging on the wall at the Kenwood Bar was a hat for every neighborhood guy in uniform.

Rain or shine, onlookers jockeyed for a view as ranks of soldiers, sailors and marines, as well as WAVES and WACS (350,000 women volunteered for the military during World War II), marched up Woodward Avenue in their tight formations. Rolling along with them were locally manufactured trucks and jeeps, often maintained by mechanics from the Dearborn Naval School or another of the area's technical academies. "V" emblems and red, white and blue bunting accented most buildings. Patriotism in all things was the rage.

A male who appeared to be able-bodied and did not serve was looked on with suspicion, even if he had been duly granted a deferment by his draft board. The stigma added to guilt many carried about not joining their brothers in the combat zone. Detroiter Philip Levine conveyed this sense in his poem "During the War."

Fedoras on the wall at the Kenwood Bar, one for each of the neighborhood boys in uniform. *Courtesy Reuther Archives.*

*I stood in a long line waiting for bread. The woman
behind me said it was shameless, someone as strong
as I am still home, still intact while her Michael was
burning to death.*

*Yes, she could feel the fire, could smell his pain all
the way from Tarawa—or was it Midway?—and he
so young, younger than I who was only fourteen.*

There were concerns that Detroit's downtown skyline, constructed during the boom years of the 1920s, might be a tempting target for Axis war planes. Security was increased at most high-rises, including Wirt Rowland's Penobscot Building, at forty-seven stories the tallest skyscraper outside New York and Chicago. P-51 Mustang fighters kept watch on it from above. The army commandeered the thirty-six-floor Union Guardian Building, another

Rowland deco masterpiece, for use as its command headquarters, overseeing manpower and ordnance matters for the entire region.

Soldiers were billeted at locations all around the city. Some were housed at old Fort Wayne by the river, which served also as the supply depot through which every locally manufactured tank, shell and spare part began its long journey to a war front. The army also stationed men at the State Fairgrounds on Eight Mile, where conditions were especially primitive. Troops slept in unheated sheds normally reserved for horses, pigs and sheep. Quonset huts seemed to spring up everywhere, a signature artifact of World War II mass-produced at the Great Lakes Steel facility downriver.

Belle Isle was another wartime camp. Spectators on the U.S. and Canadian sides watched as marines in awkward-looking watercraft (some manufactured in Michigan) conducted landing exercises along its muddy banks. By the final months of the war, some were calling the park Bella Jima. The training included men attached to the Brodhead Naval Armory on East Jefferson, scene of the pro boxing debut of native son Joe Louis just a few years earlier.

Brodhead was an art object as well as a military installation, renowned for its floor and wall tiles (fired in the kilns of the nearby Pewabic Pottery workshop) as well as for its colorful (and, some thought, *off-color*) WPA murals depicting sailors on shore leave. Detroit-based wives and girlfriends kept busy there as uniformed "anchorettes," hosting fundraisers, organizing blood drives and providing entertainment for naval personnel in local hospitals.

"Shakedown" runs for freshly minted bombers, Curtiss P-40 Warhawk fighters tearing across the sky—these were part of life in wartime Detroit. The ear-splitting noise and rattling windows they produced were frightening and comforting at the same time. The more daring pilots liked to brag about flying *under* the Ambassador Bridge, a rite-of-passage maneuver much admired despite its lack of official sanction.

American and Free French airmen were based at Selfridge Field and Willow Run to the west of the city. Female pilots (WASPS) ferrying planes to their stateside destinations operated out of Romulus Field. And 1,800 RAF flyers lived, more or less harmoniously, with their Yank cousins at the naval training center on Grosse Ile.

Fort Wayne and the fairgrounds were home also to hundreds of Italian soldiers who had surrendered en masse in the North African desert campaigns of 1942–43. They were among a group of five thousand processed through Camp Custer near Battle Creek and dispersed to facilities throughout Michigan. Detroit's Italians lived under minimum security and were assigned to construction projects and other light manual labor, their earnings redeemable for extra food and cigarette rations at the camp canteen.

Guards were struck by the good cheer with which the Italians went about their business. The truth was that, almost to a man, they were relieved to be thousands of miles and an ocean away from *Il Duce*'s lunatic war. In their free time, they tended gardens, painted murals, played and sang music. They set up camp barbershops and haberdasheries, organized holiday meals, took classes in English and conducted democratic elections to choose their own leaders.

The Italians knew that they had been rescued by their supposed adversaries, and they showed their gratitude in a variety of ways. Crumpled black-and-white newspaper photos of FDR could be seen tacked to the walls above their bunks, along with graffiti tributes to the Statue of Liberty and Old Glory. These reluctant warriors liked their taste of New World freedom, and when the fighting ended, many pursued American citizenship.

THEIR STORIES
ARE FINISHED

Anxious Detroit families kept abreast of the war's progress, and at least the general whereabouts of their servicemen, by reading magazine weeklies such as *Time, Life, Collier's* and the *Saturday Evening Post*, as well as the city's big daily newspapers, the *News, Times* and *Free Press*. The appetite for information was insatiable. Extra editions hit the streets all the time, and newsstands and cigar stores downtown bulged with periodicals of every description.

Ernie Pyle's syndicated dispatches for *Scripps-Howard* and Bill Mauldin's cartoons of the dog-faced GIs Willie and Joe, reprinted from the army newspaper *Stars and Stripes*, gave civilians a feel for life on the front. They portrayed war from a soldier's-eye view, with a hard-boiled realism usually filtered out by Hollywood and the OWI.

Pyle, Mauldin and their like made no effort to hide the mistakes and random accidents that happened in a war zone. Their young men aged a thousand years on one patrol, groused about K-rations, cursed their officers and equipment and envied the folks back home for their comfort and their complacency. They absorbed defeats and sometimes even fled in panic as their lines collapsed. And they died, in obscene numbers, often in less-than-glorious circumstances.

"In the magazines war seemed romantic and exciting, full of heroics and vitality," Pyle pecked out on his portable typewriter while embedded with an infantry unit slogging its way through the rugged country of southern Italy.

Yet I didn't seem capable of feeling it. Certainly there were great tragedies, unbelievable heroism, even a constant undertone of comedy. But when I sat down to write, I saw instead men…suffering and wishing they were somewhere else…all of them desperately hungry for somebody to talk to besides themselves, no women to be heroes in front of, damned little wine to drink, precious little song, cold and fairly dirty, just toiling from day to day in a world full of insecurity, discomfort, homesickness and a dulled sense of danger.

"I knew of only twice that the war would be romantic to the Men," Pyle concluded. "Once when they could see the Statue of Liberty and again on their first day back in the hometown with the folks."

On occasion, the stateside press carried field reports filed by women. Journalist Marjorie Avery described the sad panorama she witnessed from a pier on the English coast just after D-Day. Landing craft from the Allied armada were coming and going at a busy pace. Many arriving boats limped in, taking on water through shell holes and groaning with the weight of casualties. Avery's account, given page-one treatment by the *Detroit Free Press*, is as timeless and grimly poetic as anything written by Pyle, or even Hemingway:

Some of the men who made the first assault on the coast of France have returned. Some of them tell stories. These are the ones who walk off the ships with head, arm, hand or shoulder bandages. They tell of the battle as each saw it, of waves beating on the sands, of murderous cross-fire on the beaches, of shells exploding in air, of pain and fear, of grotesque details that leave impressions when death is all around. Some joke and say they're going back. Some, too dazed to smile, tell you stories in dull voices. They are eager for human contact and want me to write down their names for the papers. They ask how the war is going in France, just as I asked them. None knows.

Some of the men coming back aren't talking. They are carried off the ships on stretchers, bits of their clothing lying pathetically across their blanketed figures. A few look at the sky with unseeing eyes. Some are coming back who will never talk again. Their stories are finished. They come off the ships last, still figures covered with blankets and loaded like their dying brothers into waiting ambulances.

Barrage balloons ride nervously over the big blue LST boats docking at this port. The job of unloading has been going on all morning and will go on all afternoon. It is a slow, painstaking task. The port and the men who are doing the work are very quiet. There is no break in the stillness except for sudden shouted orders which are muted by the sounds of the surf.

As the ambulances roll up from the wharves to the main road above the harbor, they meet another convoy coming down—a long line of men and tanks and trucks. The men who move into war are as silent as those who are coming out.

The *Michigan Chronicle* carried news about African American soldiers too often ignored by the "mainstream" press. In one typical dispatch, a correspondent lauded the heroism of the "Negro" troops he had seen under fire in France. "Everywhere I go," he observed with pride, "are tales of our lads who waded ashore in water up to their knees to take part in the assault that forced Jerry from his strong points."

Black sailors, infantrymen and Seabees in the Pacific displayed similar courage. As their trials mounted, however, these young men ended up in the same condition as their white counterparts: "tired, wet, miserable, homesick." Still, morale stayed high, and there was always *some* good news to celebrate, even if it was just a break in the weather. Members of the black Ninety-ninth Fighter Squadron in Italy could not contain their excitement after passing a test against Axis planes with flying colors. "Like football players bursting into a dining room after a triumph," a journalist who lived among them wrote, "war-weary pilots were jubilant in their description of victories over the *Luftwaffe*."

TELENEWS

Civilians had other ways of tracking the fortunes of their loved ones abroad. Families pored over precious V-mail correspondence, which arrived irregularly and often in heavily censored form. Neighbors read letters over and over to one another, and a long gap was cause for sleepless nights.

Soldiers writing to their sweethearts were advised to keep their words brief and nonspecific. "Tell Her You Love Her—That's All She Needs to Know!" advised one barracks poster. Civilians back home got the same message. In the government pamphlet *What the Boys Want to Know*, "Keep 'Em Smiling" was the watchword, and in that vein it was almost always best to withhold troubling information. Among the guide's suggestions:

—Talk About Them. *Sure, you'd like to see them in their uniforms. Bet all the girls admire them. How is the food? What about entertainment? Taking in all the shows in camp and painting the town red when on leave? Wish you could see them!*

—The Family's Fine. *Everyone is in good health, and the old, familiar ailments are much improved.*

—And Busy, Too. *Tell them how each member of the family is working hard to help win the war quickly. And sharing a part in Civilian Defense and other wartime activities.*

—What About the Children? *Are they collecting scrap metals and otherwise assisting in the war effort?*

—Pets Make Good Reading, Too. *Describe the dog's scrapes, the cat's pranks, the canary's songs. They're all important!*

Along with the rest of the country, Detroiters turned to radio for war news. Edward R. Murrow was the best known of the correspondents invited regularly into their homes, his severe, clipped reports from the *London Blitz* somehow reassuring even as they were being punctuated by wailing sirens, *ack-ack* guns and the mournful chimes of Big Ben.

It was compelling theater. The "Murrow Boys" of CBS—H.V. Kaltenborn, Eric Severeid, Charles Collingwood, William Shirer and the young Walter Cronkite—were the vanguard of a remarkable generation of journalistic pioneers. Their commentary on military and diplomatic maneuverings in the lead up to war drove home the fragility of American security. As Geoffrey Perrett has written, "Radio alone was able to keep pace with the lurching changes of speed and direction of this helter-skelter kind of war where countries were conquered in days or hours." Once the United States was in the fray, the correspondents donned steel helmets to follow the action up close, giving their accounts of beach landings and bombing runs an immediacy unprecedented in the history of combat reportage. As the end approached, they were groping for words to describe the indescribable: liberated death camps, cities vaporized by atomic bombs.

Newsreels were another staple of the wartime information diet, packaged doses of "reality" mixed in between the travelogues, serials and *Tom and Jerry* cartoons that preceded the main feature at every movie house.

On Valentine's Day 1942, the double doors of the blue and orange streamline *moderne* Telenews Theater opened out for the first time onto Woodward Avenue, in the heart of Detroit's Grand Circus entertainment district. Designed by architect Cyril Edward Schley, it was part of a chain of venues that ran only newsreels, on a schedule fit to the needs of swing and "graveyard"-shifters. Hollywood swashbuckler Tyrone Power emceed the gala dedication, highlighted by a salute to new recruits from the Detroit Naval District training center. Under a convex glass globe of the earth, the marquee trumpeted stories like "Singapore Under Siege" and "Dorothy Lamour Sells War Bonds."

People flocked to Telenews, eager to follow international developments abroad (and perhaps even pick their boy out of a crowd) via the Movietone reels produced by the Fox and Hearst news services—narrated by Lowell Thomas, a voice as familiar as Murrow's. They watched documentaries like John Huston's *Battle of San Pietro* and Frank Capra's *Why We Fight* series. And they relied on *The March of Time* and *Pathe News* shorts, the latter always introduced by an onscreen crowing rooster.

Telenews Theater. "A Well-Informed Public Is America's Best Defense." *Courtesy Michael Hauser.*

At the center of the lobby (or News Foyer, as it was called) was a teletype machine chattering out late-breaking war bulletins. In the basement was a reading library and a booth for WXYZ Radio, with benches provided for those who wanted to watch its broadcasts live.

A product of its times, Telenews operated by a civic-minded motto so earnest that it seems corny today: "A Well-Informed Public Is America's Best Defense." The proprietors took their mission seriously, however, and in so doing profoundly shaped the way Detroiters experienced the twists and turns of the war.

FIGHTING JIM CROW
IN UNIFORM

Most symbolic of the sacrifices made for the nation's defense were the small Blue Star flags adorning front doors and windows throughout the city, the indication that a member of that household was away in the service. The stars turned gold when word came, in the form of the dreaded short telegram ("Regret to Inform…"), that a father, son or brother was not coming back. To those who passed by, they were a reminder of the price of war and a spur to even greater dedication—to the job, to conservation efforts, to *anything* that might hasten the hour when the guns would fall silent.

Despite the discrimination they often faced, Detroit's Jewish community produced more than its share of war heroes. Sixteen-year-old Rudy Newman talked his mother into signing the form vouching that he was seventeen—the minimum age for the army air corps. It was a commonplace deception, testifying to the eagerness of youngsters who barely shaved to get into the action. Newman was decorated for his valor flying F6F Hellcats against Japanese fighters. Marine William Weinstein was in the Pacific, too, earning a Purple Heart and Bronze Star for his actions at Iwo Jima. Second Lieutenant Raymond Zussman of Hamtramck received the Congressional Medal of Honor, posthumously, in recognition of his leadership with a tank battalion in southern France.

Milton Steinhardt's problem was the opposite of the one teenagers like Rudy Newman faced—he was too *old* for the service, by a good margin. But with repeated tries, he found a way to enlist. "I was alert to the danger of Hitler," Dr. Steinhardt recalled of his attitude at the time. Soon he was stepping off an LCVP into the killing zone of Omaha Beach. Eventually, his division fought all the way into Germany, where it helped liberate survivors of a concentration camp.

In common with their Jewish brothers, African Americans faced special obstacles in their efforts to serve flag and country. Even in a war waged to vindicate human rights, Jim Crow segregation was rigidly enforced—in civilian life and in the military.

At first, ministers, business leaders and members of the black press were optimistic that America's showdown with fascism would bring about an end to a system whose slights and hazards were often invisible to whites. For his part, President Roosevelt sent all the right signals. "We must be particularly vigilant against racial discrimination in any of its ugly forms," he told Congress in his 1942 State of the Union speech.

Prospects for an improvement in race relations seemed brighter than at any time since Reconstruction. "The very character of this war for freedom, for democracy, for liberation, has of necessity produced profound changes in our own thinking and has accelerated the hopes of all of us for a new America, and a new world," declared the *Michigan Chronicle*.

Change *was* coming, but its pace was much slower than it should have been. Despite pressure from Mrs. Roosevelt and other racially progressive members of his inner circle, FDR's actions on civil rights never matched his rhetoric. He feared, with good reason, a revolt by the segregationist wing of his party if he moved too directly against Jim Crow, just the kind of political trouble he did not need in the middle of a world war. In his mind, social reforms, no matter how worthy or overdue, had to be subordinated to a single-minded focus on victory over the Axis.

White supremacy continued, and not just in the South, even as American soldiers fought and died against enemies pledged to various "master race" ideologies. Two and a half million African Americans went into the service. Many were following the lead of Joe Louis, Detroit's "Brown Bomber." On recruiting posters in black neighborhoods, Joe was portrayed as a model of selfless patriotism, trading in the advantages of his civilian life for a sergeant's pay in the army.

But once in the military, they found themselves targeted for all kinds of insults and abuse. Blacks in uniform were restricted mostly to quartermaster jobs in rear areas, as cooks, bakers, launderers, truck drivers and stevedores. In all cases, they operated under the supervision of white officers.

It was supposed to be different for Frank Moody and the Tuskegee Airmen. Chosen for their elite skills, they knew from the start that everyone was watching—those expecting them to fail, as well as those who wished them well. Even for these pilots, the shadow of Jim Crow was ever-present. By order of the base commander, they could not enter the officers' club at Selfridge to get a glass of beer. Violations were punishable by court-martial. "[T]hey would take one end of the barracks, and put a couple of chairs in it as a club for black officers," Airman Lowell Steward remembered in Studs Terkel's oral history *The Good War*.

Off-duty, the Tuskegee men could not gain admission to a "whites only" USO dance. They could not sit at a soda counter at Cunningham's Drugs, and they could not go into bowling alleys, skating rinks or public swimming pools except on days and at times expressly (and often reluctantly) reserved for "Negroes."

In Detroit, there were separate hotels for whites and blacks, separate churches, hospitals and dental clinics. The rules prevented "colored" nurses from treating white servicemen. And the American Red Cross even separated its stock of blood supplies according to the race of the donor—a practice driven by prejudice, not by medical science. Some blacks tore up their pledge cards in disgust when they learned about the policy. Charles

Impatient to "get their wings," pilots from the 332nd Air Squadron take a classroom break. *Courtesy Selfridge Air Museum.*

Drew, the African American physician who developed a process for the long-distance transport of plasma, resigned from the organization in protest.

Like other black and minority soldiers, Frank Moody risked his life for a country that denied him full citizenship. His sacrifice, which was total, was part of a larger struggle to make sure that when peace returned, the ideals of equal opportunity would not be discarded as they always had been in the past. Lieutenant Moody and men like him were shock troops in what the *Pittsburgh Courier* called the "Double Victory" campaign, the fight to overcome fascism abroad and the scourge of racism at home.

PART III
EVERYDAY LIFE IN THE
ARSENAL OF DEMOCRACY

OPEN ALL NIGHT

Detroit, where they stand in line for a glass of beer…where more dames wear slacks than in Hollywood, where somebody made a mistake and a race riot resulted…where everybody has two sawbucks to rub against each other. Detroit, the hottest town in America…Baghdad on Lake Michigan.
—Hollywood Daily Variety, *October 1943*

Throughout its history, Detroit has presented two faces to the popular imagination. On the one hand, it is seen as a "wide-open" city, a haven for gangsters, grifters, bootleggers and anybody else looking for a fast dollar. On the other is a more representative city, one of manicured lawns, upright morals and a blue-collar devotion to honest work.

The reporter quoted above (whose sense of geography was shaky, at best) was trying to describe for his readers the combustibility of this stew, never more pronounced than during the boom years of the Second World War. Mayor Edward Jeffries likened his job to presiding over "a frontier town of the gold rush period," and there were days when he wondered if it was ungovernable.

People old enough to remember wartime Detroit emphasize its "24-hour-ness," the relentless bustle and flow of activity that came with hordes of second- and third-shifters, many of them recent arrivals. They recall, too, how the war intruded into every aspect of their lives, often without warning—as when the police made their sweeps of taverns and restaurants to check on draft cards.

Cultures collided, the future seemed up for grabs, everything was in a state of change. Yet people did their best to establish a degree of normalcy in the whirlwind. They showed up on time at work, raised families, went to church and now and then treated themselves to a good time—even as the distant war rumbled on, month upon month, year after year.

As a crossroad of influences, Detroit boasts a musical tradition as rich and varied as that of any city in the country. The war years were a golden age in that lineage, and to borrow a phrase from the time, "the joint was jumpin'"—everywhere, all of the time.

Outside densely packed *taquerias* in the *barrio* of southwest Detroit, a hybrid of mariachi and swing could be heard on any given night. In Dearborn, young Arab Americans found themselves caught between worlds, drawn to the novel sounds of the movies and radio even as they kept alive the music and dance traditions of their parents at weddings and other festive occasions. The three thousand or so residents of Detroit's Chinatown, then centered on Michigan Avenue and Third, celebrated New Year's and other holidays in like fashion.

The Detroit Symphony continued its performances uninterrupted throughout the war. Free outdoor concerts at the State Fairgrounds and Belle Isle were a particular highlight for families in the summer. As men departed for the service, the DSO began to feature more female musicians. Programs emphasized patriotic themes, paying special homage to American composers from Sousa and Scott Joplin to Gershwin and Aaron Copeland.

In their migration north, African Americans brought with them the ingredients for jazz, rhythm and blues and boogie-woogie. At night spots like the Blue Bird Inn on Tireman, the Flame Show Bar on John R and Baker's Keyboard Lounge at Eight Mile and Livernois, up-and-coming talents like Milt Jackson and Tommy Flanagan honed their craft in front of attentive, enthusiastic audiences.

Downtown, there was the posh Cliff Bell's on Park Avenue, known for its polished mahogany walls and air-conditioning. Similarly, the Famous Door on Griswold and dozens of other clubs offered atmosphere and music for every taste. After hours in some of them, one could hear the bleats and blasts of be-bop, an improvisational style being invented by young players bored with the tight structures of swing.

There were several impressive ballrooms in the city, among them the Crystal on Woodward and the Grande on the west side, the latter widely remembered today for the rock-and-roll concerts it hosted a generation later. Billing itself as "Detroit's Most Beautiful Dance Rendezvous," the Vanity featured Mayan Revival décor and a five-thousand-square-foot maple floor built atop weight-sensitive springs. These gave Lindy-hoppers and Jitterbuggers the "bounce" they needed to really let go.

Dan Austin, author of *Forgotten Landmarks of Detroit*, gives us a tour of the Vanity in its heyday:

> *The dance floor had two long bars, an enormous cloakroom, a bandstand, a soda fountain and a revolving chandelier with light-reflecting mirrors. The Vanity did not sell alcohol, instead offering ginger ale and juices for a dime. Everything from the light fixtures to the curtain behind the stage had an Aztec- or Maya-inspired design. The latter featured a scene of the temples at* Chichen Itza. *A huge blade sign, spelling out "VANITY" in bold vertical letters and dancing horizontally below it, hung over the East Jefferson side and let Detroiters know where the action was.*

As teenagers, Theresa Binno and her friends frequented all of the city's big ballrooms. It was good, clean fun. "We'd go in the early evening and spend three or four hours dancing, drinking Cokes," she told Austin. "I said I'd never get married unless the guy knew how to dance. It was a great time to be young."

The crown jewels of Detroit's music and dance culture were the monumental Paradise Theatre and Graystone Ballroom, both on Woodward Avenue. The Paradise was Orchestra Hall until 1939, when the DSO left for cheaper rent down the street at the Masonic Temple. After sitting vacant for two years, it was reborn as a showcase for top-flight jazz and swing.

The Paradise was an immediate success, providing black audiences in particular with "one of the finest theatres in the country not excepting the Apollo in New York City and the Regal in Chicago," according to the *Michigan Chronicle*. At the gala opening on Christmas Eve 1941, Louis Armstrong played to a packed house, and three months later Cab Calloway established a new box office record with forty thousand tickets sold in a single week.

Distinguished by its ornate balconies and a sixty-foot-high domed ceiling, the nearby Graystone offered Detroiters an equal level of entertainment. The big bands of all the greats took to its stage, among them those led by Duke Ellington, Harry James and Benny Goodman, Glen Miller, Count Basie and the Dorsey Brothers. Singing legends Ella, Billie and Lena Horne performed there, too.

The dance floor at the Graystone was said to accommodate three thousand people, but to the fire marshal's dismay, many more squeezed in on boisterous Saturday nights during the war. Ginger ale—the drink of choice at this alcohol-free venue—came fresh from the Vernor's plant next door.

Though the music being played was largely African American in inspiration, the color line remained strictly in force in Detroit, at establishments large and small. There were a few integrated "black and tan" clubs, but they were word-of-mouth affairs and kept a low profile.

Jim Crow dictated too the accommodations open to acts passing through. The biggest white performers stayed at one of the luxury hotels downtown, the Statler or perhaps the Book-Cadillac. Elite "Negro" acts (who regularly entertained in front of all-white audiences) found lodgings at the swank Gotham Hotel in "Paradise Valley," a vibrant stretch of Hastings Street bordering on the Black Bottom district on the city's lower east side. They were received like royalty as they made the rounds of the area's many black-owned restaurants, haberdasheries, drugstores and barbershops.

"The Graystone Ballroom and the [outdoor] Graystone Gardens was where we went on Monday nights, the only nights colored people could go," Motown Records founder Berry Gordy once recalled in an interview. "That was our night. Everybody who was anybody would be there, dressed to kill." There were places to show off during the rest of the week on the Valley's main drag, including the Horse Shoe Bar, El Sino and the Three Sixes.

For a small cover charge, Lars Bjorn and Jim Gallert tell us in *Before Motown*, patrons at the Club Congo got an elaborate floor show with "a headline act, chorus girls, a comedian, one or two 'not ready for headline status' acts, and music for dancing." The program lasted about an hour and changed twice a month. All terms of employment for the performers were controlled by the American Federation of Musicians, Local 5. "We worked from nine to two, seven nights, matinee on Sunday," bassist Al McKibbon remembered of those days. "I think I got paid $17.50 per week."

Radio fare during World War II tended toward buoyantly upbeat numbers like "Is You Is or Is You Ain't My Baby," "I Got a Gal in Kalamazoo," "The Chattanooga Choo-Choo," Ella's "Don't Sit Under the Apple Tree" and Nat Cole's hip anthem for the times, "Straighten Up and Fly Right." Brazilian *samba* was a particular favorite among dancers, who moved to the rhythms of "Tico Tico" and "Rum and Coca-Cola." There were also patriotic novelties with brash humor like "Get Out and Dig, Dig, Dig (Your Victory Garden)," "Praise the Lord and Pass the Ammunition" and "Pistol-Packin' Mama." Someone even came up with a "Victory Polka."

Irving Berlin, the dean of Tin Pan Alley composers, "mass-produced" his share of lightweight ditties with tongue-in-cheek lyrics, too. But sometimes he reached for something deeper, as in "This Time":

This time we will all make certain
that this time is the last time!

For this time we are out to finish
the job we started then.

Clean it up for all time this time
so we won't have to do it again!

There was an abundance of sentimental music on the radio, as might be expected in a time of separations and yearnings for home. Favorites in this category included "I'll Be Seeing You," "We'll Meet Again" and Berlin's instant standard from 1942, "White Christmas," crooned with reassuring warmth by Bing Crosby. It sold one million copies in sheet music alone.

Southern whites brought their music to Detroit, too—a mix of country, blues and gospel. Rowdy honky-tonks were springing up all over the city even before the war, catering to homesick factory workers suddenly flush with cash. In 1939, a duo from Kentucky, the York Brothers, entered tiny Universal Studios on East Jefferson and recorded "Hamtramck Mama," a throwaway "hillbilly blues" recounting the adventures of a high-living Rosie the Riveter. Within months, it was in heavy rotation on every jukebox in town.

She's a Hamtramck Mama,
and she sure does know her stuff,

She's the hottest thing in town,
Lordy how she can love!

She's truckin' in the daytime,
shimmy's at night,

She's a Hamtramck Mama
and she shakes it right

The mayor of Hamtramck, a "city within a city" of forty-seven thousand mostly conservative Polish Catholics, did not appreciate the risqué humor. He pushed through an emergency ordinance banning its play in his jurisdiction, but the move only increased the notoriety and appeal. More than 300,000 copies sold—some of them, no doubt, under the table in Hamtramck's thriving black market.

No one was more surprised by the song's commercial success than the Yorks, and their example bred a host of imitators. The joke was getting old, however, and response to their follow-up "Highland Park Mama" proved disappointing. Soon shortages of shellac and other materials shut down such mom-and-pop recording enterprises.

Music was a recognized morale-builder for the men in uniform, and civilians generously donated records from their private collections for use on bases, ships and airfields and in USO canteens and hospitals, stateside and abroad. "Here's Your Chance to Help a Wounded Service Man," declared the *Detroit News* in its campaign to gather 78-rpm discs for the military. Readers were assured that pains had been taken to identify the styles the boys wanted to hear. Their answers to a survey ran the gamut, from swing and rhythm and blues to country, from "hot bands" to "the best in the world of harmony."

Books were solicited in the same spirit. They were a cheap and portable escape from the rigors of life in uniform, in the boredom of rear areas and the tension of places where the bullets flew. The Detroit Public Library and its neighborhood branches organized several successful "victory book" drives during the war, inspired by the conviction that their importance went beyond their therapeutic value. They were, as President Roosevelt himself declared, "weapons" in a "war of ideas," one that pitted democratic free expression against the book-burning thuggery of the fascists.

AT THE MOVIES

Hollywood played a conspicuous role in sustaining homefront morale during World War II. In Detroit, the biggest movie palaces—the Fox (capacity five thousand), Michigan, United Artists, Adams and Madison—sat clustered together in the Grand Circus entertainment district on the north edge of downtown. Thirty-five cents secured entry into the fantasy of exotic grandeur each theater cultivated in its own way. Visitors marveled at the French or Italian Renaissance décor in the lobbies, accented with crystal chandeliers, thickly carpeted staircases and marble columns trimmed in gold leaf. Even the powder rooms and smoking lounges were luxurious. The four-story, 3,346-seat Hollywood Theatre on Fort Street afforded residents of southwest Detroit the same experience.

These cathedrals of excess were a respite from the gray austerity that prevailed outside their walls. During summer, a lot of people paid their money just to beat the heat. "In those days, you picked the theater with the air-conditioning," a downriver man told Dan Austin. "You didn't care what the movie was."

As show time approached, every effort was made to ramp up the crowd's anticipation. Down in front, an orchestra struck up a medley of old favorites to set the mood, or a Mighty Wurlitzer or Barton organ ascended to stage level and thundered into action, shaking the building to its foundations.

Clark Gable, Jimmy Stewart and dozens of other leading Hollywood figures enlisted for the service, and civilians monitored their activities closely. Meanwhile, Judy Garland, Mickey Rooney, Carole Lombard, Betty

Grable, the Andrews Sisters and a cavalcade of other stars made regular appearances in Detroit to promote war bonds, available for purchase at a special booth in the theater lobby. They sold for $18.75 each, maturing to a value of $25.00 in ten years.

When he wasn't overseas, Bob Hope was on stage offering wry commentary on the tire shortage, trends in women's fashions and other wartime preoccupations. Kate Smith, the leather-lunged "Songbird of the South," emerged as a national phenomenon during the war, bringing houses to their feet with her booming renditions of "God Bless America."

And the live shows by Frank Sinatra, Hoboken's rail-thin "boy next door" with the dreamy voice, provoked bedlam among his army of young female fans. These were the screaming, ecstatic "bobby-soxers" who queued around the block, surging past police lines to get closer to the object of their desire. "Not since Valentino had an entertainer been so adored," Geoffrey Perrett has written. "Their elders were variously worried and bemused… [W]herever Sinatra went the prospects of riot were strong. Windows were often smashed; fistfights would break out; there would be a trail of hospital cases. What other private citizen needed a squad car full of policemen to accompany him everywhere?" Jealous boyfriends were less impressed, noisily questioning the legitimacy of "Swoonatra's" 4-F draft status.

For most Detroiters, it was an easy walk or bus or streetcar ride to one of the more than one hundred theaters that saturated the city. There were of course cutbacks due to the war. The wattage on the façade outside was reduced to save electricity, and the buildings were modified in all kinds of ways. In early 1942, the marquee at the west side Redford Theatre came down along with its heavy iron supports, on the way to the nearest scrap yard.

But the Redford and most other houses stayed open for business. The seats inside were still plush, the popcorn tasted good (even without butter) and going to the show was a chance for people to get out of the house and socialize with friends. Youngsters sat behind ticket windows, sold concessions and worked as ushers (or "usherettes"), smart in their in caps and crisp uniforms, flashlights in hand as they patrolled the aisles. An untold number of teenagers stole their first kiss in the darkened upper reaches of the balcony.

What was projected on the screen made good on the promise of a few hours away from life's concerns—and reassurance that the good guys always triumphed over the bad. In Technicolor cartoons, Clark Kent shed his civvies to become Superman and went to work plugging volcanoes, corralling runaway trains and upending the schemes of treacherous Japateurs (who, following the wartime stereotype, were always buck-toothed and thickly bespectacled).

Popeye enlisted in the U.S. Navy. On the brink of defeat, he downed his spinach, and it was curtains for enemy torpedo boats and dive-bombing Zeroes. Warner Brothers stalwarts Bugs Bunny and Daffy Duck, hardly heroic types before the war, now outwitted monocled Nazis and made sure they were good and clobbered by the end of the reel—to the whistles and catcalls of children and adults alike. The same formula applied to the low-budget serials of the day starring Batman, the Masked Marvel and Secret Agent X-9. Even Hopalong Cassidy and Tarzan got into the act, coming out on top every time in their battles with fascist spies.

Feature films of the war years were mostly escapist in nature—period swashbucklers, westerns and romantic comedies, the slapstick of Abbott and Costello in *Buck Privates*, the breezy *Road* movies of Hope and Crosby, rousing musicals like *Anchors Aweigh* and Berlin's *This Is the Army*—all duly screened for content by the Office of War Information's Bureau of Motion Pictures. They were digested and then quickly forgotten once the patrons hit the exits.

An exception to this generally lightweight fare was Charlie Chaplin's *The Great Dictator* (1940), a shot across the Axis bow on the eve of the war that, in an industry allergic to controversy (and fearful of alienating foreign markets), could only have been made by a figure of his stature. Defying expectations, audiences turned out in droves to howl at its spot-on mockery of Hitler and Mussolini.

To preempt government censorship, the heads of the motion picture companies agreed to police themselves, making sure that "defeatist" themes and images of dead or grievously wounded (American) soldiers never made it to the neighborhood screen. Richard Lingeman cites an industry memorandum urging studios to imprint a positive, upbeat mood onto every script, capped off by an unambiguously happy ending. Among its suggestions:

> *At every opportunity, naturally and inconspicuously, show people making small sacrifices for victory—making them voluntarily, cheerfully and because of the people's own sense of responsibility, not because of any laws.*
>
> *For example, show people bringing their own sugar when invited out to dinner, carrying their own parcels when shopping, traveling on planes or trains with light luggage, uncomplainingly giving up seats for servicemen or others traveling on war priorities.*

"Message" films of the time included *Mrs. Miniver* (1942) starring Greer Garson and *Watch on the Rhine* with Bette Davis (1943). Each of these stories centered on a wife/mother who, with her selflessness and pluck, shelters her family from the fascist onslaught. The formula was part of an effort to ground and "de-glamorize" stars of the silver screen, especially women. Again, the idea was to promote a spirit of "we're all in this together" teamwork. *Daily Variety* commented on the new rules:

> *No longer are actresses pictured as leisurely, luxury-loving dolls. Today's femme star or player is as virile as the men—shown washing dishes in canteens, sweeping, hefting five-gallon coffee cans, doing hundreds of other things to prove she can take it, that she's doing her share in the war effort. Jewels, clothes, luxury are out. The screen lady today is war conscious.*

Agents and producers knew that their actors were role models, perhaps more than ever with the dislocations of war. Since everyone seemed to have a horror story about a woman whose hair got stuck in the machinery at work, starlet sensation Veronica Lake agreed to cut back her flowing locks to a shorter, "upswept" style. The press applauded Lake's patriotism, but the more severe look spelled doom for her at the box office. Some performers could not survive without the patina of "glamour."

War movies featured proven stars like John Wayne and Errol Flynn, as well as up-and-coming actors like the rugged Robert Mitchum, who won plaudits as a squad leader on Ernie Pyle's Italian front in *The Story of G.I. Joe* (1945). With its gritty, somber realism, it was a departure in look and feel from Hollywood's usual sanitized propaganda. John Morton Blum describes the template: "A few American soldiers almost always beat fifty Japanese single-handed." Men in the field laughed at the naïveté of these films, and they certainly look dated today. But audiences at home ate them up.

War movies presented a world of unflinching, melodramatic heroism and exaggerated diversity, full of clichés reinforcing how Americans *wanted* to see their fighting men rather than how they really *were*. For audiences in multi-ethnic Detroit, the appeal of "melting pot" imagery was obvious. "[C]ombat teams were invariably composed of one Negro, one Jew, a Southern boy, and a sprinkling of second-generation Italians, Irish, Scandinavians and Poles," one film historian has observed.

Time magazine echoed Hollywood on this score, emphasizing the idea of GIs from different backgrounds—white, black and brown, farm boys and urban street kids—finding common purpose in a submarine or a foxhole. The infantry unit in one movie "sounded like the roster of an All-American eleven."

> *There were Edward Czeklauski of Brooklyn, George Pucilowski of Detroit, Theodore Hakenstod of Providence, Zane Gemmill of St. Clair, Pa., Frank Christensen of Racine, Wisconsin, Abraham Dreiscus of Kansas City. There were the older, but not better, American names like Ray and Thacker, Walsh and Eaton and Tyler. The war was getting Americanized.*

Some were offended by whitewashed portrayals of the war and took issue with the presumption that audiences could not handle an approach closer to the moral grayness of the front. To sugarcoat the truth, they insisted, was a disservice to the humanity of the soldiers. Rick Atkinson quotes combat artist George Biddle on the subject: "I wish the people at home, instead of thinking of their boys in terms of football stars, would think of them in terms of miners trapped underground or suffocating to death in a tenth-story fire. I wish, when they think of them, they would be a little sick to their stomachs."

A few Hollywood films transcended the distortions of wartime and would be considered classics in any era. Detroiters fondly remember watching tough guy James Cagney show off his singing and dancing chops in *Yankee Doodle Dandy* (1942), co-starring seventeen-year-old Highland Park native Joan Leslie. They thrilled to the sacrifice of Bogart and Ingrid Bergman in *Casablanca* (1943). ("Romantic TNT!" promised the ad in the *Free Press*.) And they sat transfixed as the murder scheme concocted by *femme fatale* Barbara Stanwyck unraveled, bit by bit, in Billy Wilder's noir masterpiece *Double Indemnity* (1944).

Moviegoing was an activity tightly woven into civilian life. "At neighborhood theatres, where bills changed three times a week," Ronald Davis has written of the war years, "families could see up to six different [features] every seven days." Business was brisk, for good films and bad, big-budget spectaculars and B-pictures alike. Ninety million Americans went to the pictures every week, a standard unmatched since.

ENEMY AGENTS?

That there would be friction between the varied cultures of Detroit during World War II should come as no surprise. Some groups were singled out because of suspicions about their loyalty. FBI raids of German and Italian American homes and businesses in 1942 yielded little in the way of contraband: some dog-eared books and pamphlets, a few swastika flags and the odd short-wave radio. For a full year after Pearl Harbor, nonresidents from these communities were classified as "enemy aliens," and as such, they had to register for special identification papers. They were subject to a nightly curfew, their mail was opened and their travel was closely scrutinized. They were prohibited from owning cameras or firearms.

Some Italian-language newspapers in Detroit expressed pride in *Il Duce*'s imperial ambitions, but this evaporated once America entered the war. Grocery store windows now "carried photographs of Roosevelt's smile where earlier Mussolini's scowl had appeared." Barbershop walls displayed framed portraits of sons in uniform, decorated with Catholic icons and American flags. Signs posted in front of houses and apartment buildings declared: "We're 100 Percent for the U.S.A.!"

German Americans faced nowhere near the level of harassment they suffered during the First World War, in part because they were a generation more assimilated—and thus more detached from identification with the old-world language and culture. Community leaders denounced Hitler, and the uniforms, salutes and theatrical goose-stepping of the local Bund embarrassed them. Men (and women) from the community enlisted for the service in impressive numbers and served with distinction on all fronts of the war.

Still, Detroiters of German ancestry felt it prudent to keep celebrations of their ethnic identity within careful limits. For its weekend beer-and-*schnitzel* sing-alongs, the Dakota Inn Rathskeller on John R dropped "Deutschland Uber Alles" in favor of "God Bless America," belted out with a fervor that would have made Kate Smith blush.

There was one "espionage" case early in the war involving elements of the local German community, farcical in retrospect but cause for alarm in the context of the times. After being shot down over Britain, a Luftwaffe pilot named Hans Krug was shipped with his unit to a POW camp in Ontario. In April 1942, Krug escaped and made his way to Windsor. From there, he paddled a stolen boat across the river to Belle Isle and then, in broad daylight, walked over the MacArthur Bridge and into the lower east side of Detroit.

Krug was taken in by Margareta Bertelmann, a German-born resident whose address he later claimed to have known from relief packages she mailed regularly to his camp. Bertelmann gave him food, clothing and a little cash before delivering him to a restaurant at Jefferson and East Grand owned by Max Stephan, a Detroiter with well-known ties to the Bund.

Stephan took his "VIP" guest around town with reckless abandon, introducing him to friends, treating him to lavish meals with plenty of locally brewed beer and even subsidizing a visit to a brothel. After several days of this conspicuous hospitality, he put Krug on a Greyhound to Chicago, the first leg of a journey to safe haven in Mexico. The FBI was watching, however, and the fugitive was intercepted in San Antonio. Arrests back in Detroit followed almost immediately.

As small as it was, the episode attracted international attention. For her part in sheltering the escaped prisoner, immigration authorities ordered Mrs. Bertelman to an enemy alien facility out of state. Stephan, meanwhile, was tried and convicted of treason, and only the eleventh-hour intervention by President Roosevelt saved him from the gallows. Whether the Krug affair amounted to anything more than a series of isolated, comic-opera incidents—whether it was a conspiracy carried out by a dedicated if inept "Nazi Spy Ring"—has never been fully resolved.

In Detroit, as elsewhere in the country, there was a campaign, scattered and uncoordinated, to purge all positive references to Japanese culture from public view. After Pearl Harbor, the Redford Theatre painted over the Kabuki murals that framed its stage, created in the more innocent 1920s when such fanciful "exotica" was wildly popular.

"SPONTANEOUS COMBUSTION"

It is a tragic paradox that racial minorities in the United States found themselves targeted for abuse during World War II. The internment of Japanese Americans in the western states and attacks on Mexican American "Zoot-suiters" in a number of big cities are but two examples of this reality. In Detroit, the most serious trouble rose out of the divide between the city's white and black residents.

Tensions in the Motor City on this front ratcheted up as half a million people migrated in from the South, factory workers of both races now suddenly jammed into uncomfortable proximity. Tempers grew short and altercations were common as people crowded into lines for just about everything. In view of the frustrations of life in wartime Detroit, some wrote the folks back home that they had landed in the "'Arsehole' of Democracy."

It was not hard to see where things were headed. A 1943 *Life* photo essay, "Detroit is Dynamite," catalogued the ominous signs, which added up to "a morale situation which is perhaps the worst in the U.S." Officials at the OWI were not happy with this level of candor on social ills, and the magazine's editors bowed to pressure to delete the article from copies sold overseas.

Others saw trouble coming, too. "We can't whip Hitler abroad and let fascism run up and down the streets of Detroit," the always-quotable congressman Adam Clayton Powell of Harlem told reporters during a visit in the spring of 1943. The *Wage Earner*, organ of the Association of Catholic Trade Unionists local, warned of a "subterranean race war" ready to boil to the surface. And NAACP director Walter White sounded the alarm after his fact-finding tour in early June 1943. "Let us drag out into the open what has been whispered throughout Detroit for months," he urged anybody willing to listen. "A race riot may break out here at any time."

Housing was in critically short supply, and competition for it led to many clashes between whites and blacks. By an unwritten code, Detroit's surging African American population was confined to Black Bottom and a few other mostly run-down residential pockets around the city. In February 1942, violent protests erupted when a group of black families challenged the rules by attempting to move into the new Sojourner Truth homes, a federally funded experiment in integrated living.

Residents from the adjacent Polish American neighborhood objected to what they saw as an invasion, a badly conceived bit of social engineering sure to bring with it soaring crime rates and collapsing real estate values. Members of a hastily organized Seven Mile–Fenelon Improvement Association flooded officials at every level with angry letters and phone calls. The intensity of the reaction was no doubt fueled by what World War II scholar John Morton Blum has identified as "the psychological impulse to ostracize those still lower on the social scale than they were."

Incendiary rhetoric from outside the area—from politicians, media personalities, even church leaders—heightened the tension. "The Sunday broadcasts over Detroit's radio stations [are] a babble of racism, fundamentalism, ignorance and guile," the *New Republic* told its readers, pointing to Father Coughlin, Gerald L.K. Smith and their demagogic imitators. "No city, North or South, could match this hellish symphony of the Detroit radio stations."

With fists clenched, placard-brandishing whites hurled rocks and epithets, terrifying their prospective new neighbors as the police escorted them away for their own protection. One sign got right to the point:

A WHITE PROJECT
FOR A
WHITE NEIGHBORHOOD

Counter-protestors who arrived to defend the tenants brought with them an equally concise message:

HITLER SUPPORTS
HOUSING DISCRIMINATION

Seeing their opportunity, elements of the KKK, a force in Detroit since the 1920s, emerged from the shadows to fan the flames. A klansman (or fellow traveler) burned a cross one night in front of the Sojourner Truth complex. The venom flowed on unchecked for weeks, and many blacks decided to drop out of the program rather than risk life and limb.

There was conflict also in the war plants. In April 1941, Ford managers at the Rouge brought in non-unionized blacks to replace white employees striking for collective bargaining rights. Bloody confrontations inevitably followed. Packard workers walked off their jobs when a handful of African Americans were promoted to supervisory positions. The UAW denounced such "hate strikes," and an equal-opportunity rally it sponsored in Cadillac Square drew an integrated crowd of ten thousand. But disruptions continued, reflecting a hard core of opposition to any changes in the racial status quo.

Detroit's big explosion unfolded over two steamy days and nights in late June 1943. The precise origins—the spark that set off what the Department of Justice later called "spontaneous combustion"—will never be known for sure. What we can say is that here, as in so many civil disturbances, one or two minor incidents unleashed long-simmering animosities and, before anyone could stop it, spiraled into a conflagration.

As darkness approached on Sunday evening, June 20, at the end of a long day in ninety-degree heat, fistfights broke out between young black and white men packed in a gridlock of cars and bodies on the Belle Isle Bridge. Cooler heads did not prevail, and like a force of nature, the violence took on a momentum of its own, propelled by sensational (*false*) rumors as it spread into the city proper. A black man had raped a white woman, someone loudly announced. White thugs threw an African American woman and her child to their deaths in the Detroit River, others cried, with equal volume.

Adding to the bad blood that night was the presence of two hundred or so off-duty white sailors stationed at the nearby Brodhead Armory on East Jefferson. Alcohol-fueled and spoiling for a fight, they were only too happy to launch themselves into the mêlée once it came into their sights.

The police were undermanned and overwhelmed, and soon downtown itself was a war zone. The sound of broken glass filled the air, and Paradise Valley was under siege. Brandishing the crude tools of the mob—bricks, tire irons, sections of metal pipe and a few guns—gangs of white men pushed their way up Woodward Avenue, ready to attack any black person who happened to get in their way. People were pulled out of movie lines and off streetcars and savagely beaten. Motorists of both races scrambled for their

The dynamite explodes. "Bloody Monday," June 21, 1943. *Courtesy Reuther Archives.*

lives as the self-styled vigilantes overturned and torched random vehicles while bystanders cheered them on.

The scene reminded *Free Press* columnist Malcolm Bingay of episodes that haunted him from his youth in the Deep South: "On the streets of Detroit I saw again the same horrible exhibition of uninhibited hate as they fought and killed one another—white against black—in a frenzy of homicidal mania, without rhyme or reason. Their faces were all the same, their lips drawn back, their teeth bared like fangs, their eyes glazed—beastial faces bereft of all human expression."

No one knew when the chaos would end or how far the swath of destruction would reach. With loaded hunting rifles, men in the suburbs stood watch on their lawns and front porches. The commander at Selfridge ordered the Tuskegee pilots confined to the base. Meanwhile, Mayor Jeffries and Governor Harry Kelly vacillated about the next move, hoping to be somehow spared the embarrassment of calling Washington for help.

The madness rolled on through dawn, as Detroit's Bloody Sunday turned into Bloody Monday. "It was a real race riot," recalled James Cummings, an African American eyewitness. "It was not like this in 1967, where it was mostly looting. In 1943 they had boundaries set up which, if you would pass, you would certainly get killed or hurt."

For every story of the horror that unfolded in Detroit at the start of that second wartime summer, there were instances, too, of people reaching out to one another across the color line. "Riot Foes Fraternize at Hospital," the *Free Press* reported Tuesday morning, looking for signs of light amid the darkness. "Wounded Negroes and Whites Sit Side by Side as Staff Works Tirelessly." These were breaches of race etiquette similar to those occurring with more and more frequency in war zones overseas, each a spontaneous brotherhood of the wounded in which old distinctions lost their meaning. The sheer unexpectedness of these moments made them newsworthy:

> *Receiving Hospital was probably the one place in Detroit Monday where Negroes and white men met on amicable terms. Bleeding Negroes and whites sat side by side, sometimes even talking together, as the staff of 200 nurses and 60 doctors and interns battled tirelessly to staunch the flow of blood and patch up broken bodies. A few minutes earlier the injured had been the hunted or hunters in the rioting a few blocks away, but now the fight was over. Dazed and mostly silent, they sat there mopping faces with blood-tinged handkerchiefs or strips of torn shirt until the doctors could get to them.*

Alixa Naff's memoir of growing up during the Great Depression and World War II, included in the Wayne State Press anthology *Arab Detroit*, gives us a window into the day-to-day life of those years. She recalls the struggles of her Syrian-born parents to establish a foothold in the city and the excitement felt by the entire family when the prosperity they had long dreamed about finally arrived with the defense boom. Residents of their Highland Park neighborhood now had steady jobs and money to spend, and the Naffs' small grocery went from red ink to black.

They were living the American dream, able to pay cash for a two-story red-brick house on Tennyson Avenue walking distance from the store. It had a front porch with a swing, a patch of dirt in back for gardening and enough room to accommodate the relatives who were always passing through town.

But Pearl Harbor changed everything. Like millions of other families, the Naffs had to say goodbye to their young men, uncertain if they would ever see them again. Alixa's brothers George and Nick enlisted right away, against the tearful protests of their mother, Yamna. She would be consumed with worry about them for the next three and a half years. Alixa conspired with her other siblings to shield her parents from bad war news. But Yamna insisted on wearing nothing but mourning black and refused to celebrate Christmas or other holidays until her sons were safely home.

A childhood interest in maps and foreign countries earned Alixa the family nickname "Eleanor Roosevelt," after the famously well-traveled First Lady. Yamna, still rooted in the ways of the old country, was certain her daughter's brains and ambition would scare off potential suitors.

As her aging father's strength waned, Alixa took over responsibility for running the store. She remembered the regulars who used to hang around and talk, characters who made her laugh and revealed things about the world beyond Detroit they didn't teach in school. Fred Logan was a particular favorite, a tall and dignified African American who each spring would vanish for months at a time to barnstorm in the minor leagues of Negro baseball. Alixa waited eagerly for Fred's tales about life on the road.

But the lines in those days were sharply drawn, and the sight of a black man fraternizing outside his race usually attracted unwanted notice. "Fred was no loiterer," Alixa insists. "He was kind and helpful, always busying himself with chores in the store lest our white customers question his presence." He refused compensation because, he said, "her Dad had at one time helped him when he was in need."

The time in need was a Monday morning in late June 1943. "Fred rushed to the store from downtown to warn me that the rioters were marching up Woodward Avenue to connect with rioters from the Davison Avenue neighborhood of blacks," Alixa remembered. Angry voices signaled the mob's approach.

> *It was mid-afternoon.* [Fred] *helped close the store and walked me home. As it turned out, the rioters were turned back about a mile before they reached our part of Woodward. With great bravado and curiosity and even greater stupidity, I drove to Davison Avenue only to be turned around in terror by flying stones and rotten vegetables. The next day Fred scolded me about the thoughtlessness of my act.*

Alixa's father insisted that Fred lie low in the back room of the store until the danger had passed.

There were many Detroiters like the Naffs, thousands of people who offered sanctuary in their attics and garages and church basements during the riot, like a twentieth-century Underground Railroad. The rescuers helped because they saw those in peril, even strangers of a different color, as family.

"Fred was not only a protector but a friend," Alixa Naff writes of her dear Mr. Logan, a beloved big brother. "He was always welcome at our table, as a policeman who came to our back door one day discovered. The officer had been summoned by our neighbor, who saw Fred knock at our side door." In this case, the power of friendship was stronger than the prejudices of the day.

The Motor City violence did not abate until Monday evening, June 21, when the boots of six thousand federal troops hit the ground, bayonets fixed, tanks and trucks with machine guns rumbling alongside them in support. It was easy to forget that there was another, larger war going on outside the city. Belated as it was, the show of force worked, and martial law took hold. It was an eerie scene as soldiers patrolled the near-deserted streets of a place that liked to call itself the Arsenal of Democracy.

Governor Kelly instituted a nightly curfew and banned all liquor sales. Tigers games were canceled, and for days the air reeked of charred wood and tear gas. Businesses remained shuttered and schools, post offices and other municipal buildings stayed closed until further notice. Residents of Paradise Valley waited it out inside their homes as their community endured a protective lockdown.

The official death toll was thirty-four, the majority of the victims African Americans. The actual body count was almost certainly higher. Six hundred were injured seriously enough to be sent to the hospital, including a number of police officers, and the court docket for the week recorded over one thousand arrests. Property damage ran into the multimillions. And the blow to the city's image, something statistics could not measure, was grievous and lasting.

There were political casualties, too. Mayor Jeffries was eventually turned out of office, in large part because of his halting response to the days of anarchy in his city. Troops stayed in town to keep the peace for months and bivouacked on Belle Isle, on the lawn of the Detroit Public Library and any other public space that could be made to accommodate them.

The postmortems and finger-pointing started even before the smoke had cleared. Some thought a vaguely defined case of "war nerves" had caused the explosion. President Roosevelt knew it was more complex than that, but he declined to give the fireside chat on race urged by his wife and other advisors. Privately, he expressed concern about the threat to production posed by such racial disorders. Detroit's munitions output fell an estimated 6 percent during its "Bloody Week," and what happened there showed signs of becoming a national contagion. Disturbances flared up in Harlem, Chicago, St. Louis, Galveston, El Paso and dozens of other American cities over the course of that long, hot wartime summer.

The president lamented, too, the aid and comfort given the enemy by newswire photographs of rampaging mobs and overturned cars. Indeed, the strife in Detroit was a staple of German and Japanese propaganda for at least the next year. Nazi-controlled Vichy radio in France called the riot a product of "the internal disorganization of a country torn by social injustice, race hatreds, regional disputes, the violence of an irritated proletariat, and the gangsterism of a capitalistic police."

Texas congressman Martin Dies, the arch-conservative chairman of the House Un-American Activities Committee, came to a different conclusion, charging that the violence in the Motor City was the handiwork of deep-cover Japanese agents. He presented no evidence to support the theory, however.

For Aid and Comfort to the Enemy.   Courtesy PM

Race riots like the one in Detroit were grist for Axis propaganda. *Courtesy Reuther Archives.*

And inevitably, there were those eager to lay blame at the doorstep of the First Lady. Critics had long condemned what they saw as her "meddling" on race issues, and they had not forgotten the tumultuous reception she received in Black Bottom in 1935 when she turned the first shovel for the new Brewster-Douglass housing project. "In Detroit, a city known for the growing impudence and insolence of its Negro population," a letter to the Jackson, Mississippi *Daily News* declared, "an attempt was made to put your preachments into practice, Mrs. Roosevelt." Now she had "blood on her hands." Similar statements appeared throughout the southern press.

To understand what lay behind the '43 Detroit riot, however, it is not necessary to fabricate Axis provocateurs or defame crusading social reformers. The root problem was segregation and the attitudes that supported it, even in the North, even during a war fought in the name of human rights. The *real* cause was Jim Crow.

On July 24, barely a month after the rioting had subsided, CBS aired *An Open Letter on Race Hatred*, a radio play by William M. Robson challenging citizens across the country to look in the mirror as they pondered the lessons of Detroit. Though preachy in tone, it was a courageous statement for its time, one that provoked no end of criticism from those who wanted to continue sweeping the issue of America's racial divide under the rug.

"Detroit, sprawling across the flat Michigan prairie, baked in the near-vertical sun," the narrator began, setting the stage for the explosion to come. An array of voices took listeners from the traffic jam on the Belle Isle Bridge to the random, roving terror that followed. The fuel? "*Rumor!* More dangerous than dynamite! More deadly than a plague! Rumors tailor-made—one for black ears, one for white ears."

Sound effects re-created the mayhem in all its harrowing detail. The costs went beyond the pain felt by one city. One million man-hours of defense work were sacrificed on the altar of racial hatred. "How many of your sons will die for the lack of the tanks and planes and guns which Detroit did not make that day?" the narrator asked pointedly. It was cause for national shame. "We lost Bataan—gallantly. We surrendered Corregidor—with honor. We were defeated at Detroit by ourselves."

Fortunately, as we have seen, there were people in the Motor City who kept their heads and did not succumb to the furies of the mob. Robson presented a series of episodes from the riot that, taken together, brought home the point. A quick-thinking woman hides a fellow passenger under her seat as marauders sweep through their streetcar. Black and white students from

Northeastern High walk home together after graduation, their numbers a protection against harm.

And three off-duty white sailors intervene to stop a gang from accosting a black pedestrian downtown. "I'm just payin' off a debt!" one of them explained, his jaw set as he rolled up his sleeves. He was acting in the name of an African American shipmate lost in the Pacific. The hour ended with a plea for racial understanding by 1940 GOP presidential candidate Wendell Willkie.

Out of the ashes, there *were* signs of hope in Detroit. Schools and churches, UAW locals and concerned citizens throughout the city began discussions about how to prevent a relapse. An integrated crowd packed a "Double-V" rally at Olympia Stadium. And James Farmer of the Congress for Racial Equality came to town to lead a sit-in at the popular Garfield's restaurant, a tactic that looked ahead to the civil rights movement of the 1960s. In this case, nonviolence worked: after a few tense days, the owners agreed to end their longstanding "Whites Only" policy and serve customers regardless of their race. It would fall to the postwar generation to build on these isolated but important foundations.

MAKING DO WITH LESS

Everyday life in wartime Detroit involved perpetual belt-tightening and vigilance against wasting resources. To manage scarcity and control inflation, the Office of Price Administration froze prices on most consumer goods in 1942 and imposed rationing on staples whose availability had previously been taken for granted. People had to get creative in finding alternatives—or they had to do *without*.

With access to raw materials in Asia and the Pacific interrupted by Japanese conquest, it was the rubber shortage that hit Americans most immediately. Synthetics were on their way but were too early in the development stage to be adequate substitutes. Conservation was, accordingly, the order of the day on the roads and highways.

"Some seem bent on driving their tires down to the rims," a British journalist observed as he traveled around the country. "[O]thers pay exorbitant prices—$25, $50, for new ones. And others put their cars away for the duration." The shortage was the universal topic of conversation at rest stops, he noted with the bemused eyes of an anthropologist, "giving the layman-driver a weird lingo. He now…talks of such things as the fabric of a tire and the carcass, of recapping and retreading, as if they were things he learned as a tiny tot, and of the potential yield of rubber plants on the great alkali deserts."

U-boat attacks on tanker convoys crossing the Atlantic dictated equally big changes in day-to-day civilian life. To save heating oil, hotel managers, apartment building superintendents and homeowners were asked to lower thermostats in the winter, right to the edge of discomfort. Longjohns and thick wool sweaters were mandatory accessories, day and night.

Gas rationing brought with it a crackdown on careless driving practices. Washington imposed a national "Victory Speed Limit" of thirty-five miles per hour, a step that made sense on paper but was all but impossible to enforce, infringing as it did on what Richard Lingeman has described as "every American's sacred right to drive an automobile as fast and as far as he liked."

Posters warned drivers about hot-rodding and "jackrabbit" starts. "Is This Trip Necessary?" was a question to be asked before every turn of the ignition. "Hitler Smiles When You Waste Miles" was another reminder. Retail stores suspended delivery services, asking customers to find a more efficient way to get their purchases home. "Don't Delay, Buy It Today, Carry It Away" was the popular slogan.

In December 1942, the "Inquiring Reporter" column in the *Free Press* presented man-in-the-street testimonials about the effects of gas rationing. (An "A" card limited individuals to just three gallons a week.) There were challenges, but most Detroiters worked around them with stoic good humor. "If I can help win the war by shivering on a street corner, that's OK by me," said one woman who had put her car in mothballs. "These are strenuous mornings for me. I have to walk half a mile from my home to the Wilshire bus line, then transfer to a Gratiot car for a forty-five minute trip to work each day."

Attorney Frank Norris showed the same spirit. "All we use the car for is for family trips," he explained, "so it looks like we are going to do more walking." His lone regret was the need to cancel weekly visits to the Belle Isle Zoo, where his three-year-old son liked to watch the elephants. "He'll be inconvenienced," Norris said with a wink, "but he can take it."

Shortages of aluminum and other metals meant restrictions on such everyday items as typewriters, paper clips, toothpaste tubes, coat hangers, nail clippers, foil chewing gum wrappers—and alarm clocks, making punctuality an extra challenge for many war workers.

Women used toothpicks as hair pins. Low-grade materials like zinc replaced the copper in pennies and the nickel in nickels. Some coins were made out of spent shell casings.

It was calculated that thirty melted-down lipstick tubes converted into twenty rifle cartridges. Even the cannons and other antique ordnance on display in Detroit's city parks were summoned back to active duty, "repurposed" for the defense needs of a new generation.

Department stores experimented with wooden scooters, tops and other children's toys, and new bicycles were just about impossible to find. Lunchboxes were made of cheap fiberboard. Road crews covered manholes with cast concrete covers. Wartime rationing reached even to the grave and beyond, as casket manufacturers discontinued the use of bronze in their 1942 models.

Like tires, razor blades were used and re-used well beyond their normal life span. The nicks and cuts were a small price to pay for winning the war. Thirty thousand blades, an American "specialty" according to Goering, contained enough steel for fifty .30-caliber machine guns.

Perfumes and colognes were in short supply, too. An ad in a men's magazine offered this advice about how to manage the dilemma: "Avoid waste. Since there is no real substitute for *Aqua Velva*, we suggest you use it carefully. Just a few drops after shaving leave your skin tingling and refreshed."

The issue of cosmetics proved especially vexing for the (almost exclusively male) members of the War Production Board. A survey indicated that face-powder, lipstick and rouge were too critical to homefront morale to be rationed. The "lift" a woman got from her weekly visit to the beauty shop, the board concluded, meant higher spirits and optimum productivity for the entire household.

Paper was handled with unusual care during World War II and not easily consigned to the wastebasket. Greens-keepers at Detroit's public and private golf courses narrowed fairways and let the rough grow higher than prescribed by the rule book. Clubhouses limited the sale of "reprocessed" balls to two per week. "On the black market," *Time* reported, "prewar golf balls that once sold for $10 a dozen were bringing $40, $50, $60 a dozen, and were hard to get at any price."

To keep lines open for those in uniform or otherwise on official business, telegram and telephone service was deemed a privilege to be used sparingly. "Please limit your call to 5 minutes" was the curt greeting as the operator put you through to your party. A Michigan Bell ad put the matter more bluntly: "He'll drill a Jap with a long-distance call you didn't make."

During the war, clothing was homemade rather than purchased, shoes repaired rather than discarded. Worn sofas and chairs were reupholstered or covered with blankets. Men's stores along the posh "Avenue of Fashion" on Livernois sold only single-breasted suits with narrow lapels, no cuffs or pleats. Hudson's flagship store downtown opened a trousers shop just for women, offering an equally streamlined range of styles.

The "bobby sox" so popular among teenaged girls were more than a badge of belonging. The short, "bobbed" white stockings used no dye and required less cotton than the knee-length variety. World War II saw the advent of the two-piece women's bathing suit—scandalous, perhaps, but justified as a patriotic "conservation" measure.

The notorious "Zoot suit" of the war years emerged out of Mexican, African American and Italian neighborhoods, in Detroit and other cities around the country. For most of the young "hep-cats" who embraced it, the fad was a symbol of independence and harmless rebellion.

But with its long, peacock-colored coats, accessorized with billowing pegged pants and broad-brimmed hats, the style drew disapproving stares from the more conservative minded. As austerity deepened, the WPB prohibited Zoots as a waste of cloth. Those choosing to defy the ban invited trouble when they went to dance halls and night clubs on the weekend. Servicemen took them to be gang members or, even worse, draft-dodgers, and reports of violence were common.

"Use it up, wear it out, make it do or do without" was the credo for life in wartime Detroit. Out of necessity, housewives learned to do tasks formerly left to the men: repairing and maintaining automobile engines, fixing plumbing and electrical wiring, finding parts to keep the old furnace in working condition.

"Give till it hurts" was another motto. In "Victory Homes" (marked by a "V" decal on the front window) kitchenware, keys, galoshes and rain slickers were dutifully gathered up and delivered to a collection point at the neighborhood school.

Precious silk and nylon went into parachutes and tow-ropes for gliders. Some young women resorted to the expedient of "bottled stockings," a kind of make-up that fooled no one, even when the "seam" so carefully drawn up the back of the leg was relatively straight. The smears left on clothing provided incriminating evidence for parents curious about why their daughter was so late getting home from her Saturday night date.

Holidays were not exempt from the demands of war. The floats rolling down Woodward Avenue in Hudson's 1942 Thanksgiving Day extravaganza (there were no parades in '43 or '44) carried signs declaring, "I'm on my way to the Rubber Salvage!" Historian Jim Kushlan reminds us that the extended Christmas shopping season we know so well today began during the war years. In 1943, the post office announced that gift packages bound for the Pacific had to be in the mail by the end of October to ensure delivery by December 25.

OWI posters portrayed St. Nick with a markedly less jolly countenance than usual. The most famous had him decked out in a steel helmet and olive-green fatigues, accompanied by the caption "Santa Clause Has Gone to War!" Department stores hired women to don the fake beards and padded suits expected by girls and boys, whose wish lists had most definitely *not* been suspended for the duration.

Due to a shortage of shipping space on trains, Christmas trees were hard to get in the city. Families improvised substitutes that (unlike synthetic tires or bottled stockings) worked as well or better than the real thing, and departures from tradition did not faze youngsters who had never known them in the first place. Home-crafted ornaments replaced fancy tin and glass-blown German and Japanese bulbs, which were donated for salvage. Children fashioned decorations out of non-priority materials like cardboard, string and pinecones, and when mixed with water, a box of *Lux* soap powder made for a festive snow effect.

People were also creative in bartering points and ration privileges during the war. Farmers gave meat and butter allotments to their city cousins in exchange for gas tokens. Housewives traded sugar and coffee stamps to suit the specific needs of their families. Those with connections across the Detroit River sometimes supplemented their diets with contraband smuggled in through customs at the bridge and tunnel. British journalist Alistair Cooke estimated that every day two thousand people made the trip over to Ontario with the intent of bringing back beef, pork, lamb and chickens.

Most of this "under the table" maneuvering was small in scale and had a negligible effect on the war effort. Minor infractions drew at most a slap on the wrist—a citation or a fine and probably the censure of neighbors. Requests for special favors at the greengrocer or butcher shop attracted accusing looks from the other customers in line. At such moments, the words "don't you know there's a war on?" hung awkwardly in the air. Transgressors usually got the message and adjusted their behavior accordingly.

There was, however, a larger and more organized black market, one that went far beyond accepted boundaries. As one writer on the period has observed, "War does not create new problems with which we are unfamiliar. It accentuates old problems." *Greed* had not been abolished with the proclamation of the Four Freedoms, and the criminally minded could not resist the temptations presented by the national emergency.

Hoarding, profiteering, "buying from Mr. Black" (or "Mr. B.") were facts of life in every city and town in the country, including Detroit. Working with neighborhood watchdogs, the police struggled to contain the problem, with only partial success. Muckraking newspaper exposés of fencing schemes, ration-book forgery rings and smuggling networks were frequent, and readers took satisfaction when the chiselers got their just punishment.

The regimen of "Meatless Mondays" at the dinner table reminded those old enough to remember of the sacrifices of the Great War. The meat that was available was mostly the cheaper cuts. "My mother devised 900 different ways of using hamburger or chicken," Detroiter Barbara Williams recalled, not necessarily with nostalgia. Housewives and bakeries were forced to cut back on basic ingredients. Columnist Walter Winchell parodied the situation:

Roses are Red, Violets are Blue
Sugar is Sweet. Remember?

Much of what was on the plate came from a patch of dirt just outside the back door. "Remember, food is ammunition," the seed catalogues declared, and by V-J Day an estimated 40 percent of the produce consumed in American households was grown in "Victory Gardens"—twenty million all across the country. Rooftops, road medians, vacant lots and schoolyards—every bit of arable soil was subject to the shovel of the amateur farmer. Grandmother's lost arts of canning and preserving were also revived, a necessity if one was to get through the Michigan winters with proper nourishment.

"Children became acquainted with exotic new vegetables such as Swiss chard and kohlrabi, introduced because of the seed shortage," Richard Lingeman tells us. The humor editor for the *Free Press* spoke for many who longed for the prewar diet. "Funny how they never mention rationing turnips and parsnips and other things I don't like."

The paper's lifestyle page in November 1942 shared kitchen advice from housewives in Great Britain, who had longer experience in navigating scarcity. Readers were reminded that it was not too early to begin thinking about the next holiday meal:

CHRISTMAS
For HIROHITO

Having roast turkey, goose or
chicken for Christmas dinner?

Save some for the Japs!
Give them the drippings

Strain all waste kitchen fats
into a wide-mouthed can

When you have a pound,
sell it to the meat dealer

FATS MAKE

EXPLOSIVES!

Shortages affected everyday habits in all kinds of ways. To save tobacco, a lot of men abandoned smoking, or at least switched to a pipe. Those who couldn't kick the habit stood in line outside Cunningham's when word leaked of a fresh shipment of cigarettes. People pretended the ersatz coffee they gulped down on the way to work in the morning (with their toast and oleo) was the real thing.

Sanders confectionery and the local Vernor's and Faygo bottling plants experimented with a variety of sugar substitutes—with less-than-satisfactory results, if customer feedback from the time is to be believed. Devotees of Fleer's bubble gum noticed a particularly disagreeable change when the company introduced synthetic rubber into its product. "It had a grainy texture and my tongue would go right through it," one Detroit woman recalled. The Michigan Beekeepers' Association posted signs during the war reminding the public of the "strategic" value of its members' work—providing honey as a food sweetener, as well as wax for candles, engine lubrication and waterproofing. Bees were "doing their part for victory," the group declared, and to disturb the hives in any way was sabotage.

In 1942, another Detroit institution, the east-side Better Made potato chip company on Gratiot, was forced to curtail operations when the WPB classified its product as a "nonessential" food. The stakes were high in such rulings, and lobbyists from every industry competed to influence how they came out.

Among the brands granted "essential" status (and, therefore, exemption from rationing) were Coca-Cola, Wrigley's gum and Lucky Strike, Pall Mall and Camel cigarettes. Each was hailed for its "therapeutic" value in easing tensions in the defense plants, and each was included in the "K" rations of American (and British and Russian) servicemen around the globe. Needless to say, this was a coup for the companies involved, assuring them enormous markets after the war.

A turf war of sorts broke out over another part of G.I. Joe's diet: chocolate. Hershey's iconic bar ruled in most places, but its tendency to liquefy in extreme heat made it unsuitable for men stationed in the tropical climes of the Pacific. Rival candy maker Mars offered a solution with M&M's, a bite-sized confection with a melt-resistant outer shell patented in 1941. The sales pitch would achieve advertising immortality: "Melts in Your Mouth, Not in Your Hand."

Companies of all kinds "re-branded" their products, wrapping them in red, white and blue. "Don't be a public enemy!" read an ad for Kimberly-Clark. "Be patriotic and smooth sneezes with *Kleenex* to help keep colds from spreading to war workers—America needs every man—full time!"

Marketers at the United States Brewers' Association also invested their wares with a nobler wartime meaning. You can hear the swell of fife and drum as you read the copy: "In this America of tolerance and good humor, of neighborliness and pleasant living, perhaps no beverage more fittingly belongs than wholesome *beer*. And the right to enjoy this beverage of moderation—this, too, is part of our own American heritage of personal freedom."

Beginning in 1942, saloons throughout Detroit served "Victory Beer," produced locally (with "100% American ingredients") at the Koppitz family brewery near the river on Atwater. The label on each bottle featured a battlefront image—a fighter plane, tank, submarine or artillery piece, one hundred variations in all. They were instant collectors' items, and strong sales convinced Koppitz to offer another, darker wartime brew, dubbed "Black-Out Beer."

America remained a democracy, even under the pressures of war, and once in a while the public succeeded in pushing back against WPB edicts. After weeks of angry letters and telegrams, the board reversed itself on the potato chip question. Upon further consideration, the snack was now deemed a "health food," for many perhaps "the only ready-to-eat vegetable available" on a daily basis. Better Made was back in business.

Along with chip-delivery vans, the streets and alleys of wartime Detroit were alive with produce and dairy wagons, the carts of knife sharpeners and clothing peddlers and the horse-drawn ice trucks so common in the days when refrigeration was a luxury. Neighborhood kids were dispatched, usually with some protest, to shovel the manure left in their wake. On sweltering afternoons, children swarmed around the truck pleading for the ice man to chip off a few frozen slivers. In the winter, noisy coal trucks made their home-delivery rounds. The ash and dust residue was scattered to melt slippery sidewalks. *Nothing* was wasted.

"Patriotic Consumption." A label for Koppitz's "Victory Beer." *Courtesy Archives of Michigan.*

Reminders of the moral imperative to conserve were impossible to avoid during the war, even in the most unlikely, "inaccessible" places. John Morton Blum relates the story of a visiting Englishman as he settled into his seat on a commercial flight over the praries of the Midwest. "Here, if anywhere, was normality," he thought to himself as he lazily gazed out the window.

> [H]*undreds of miles of it and not a sight or a sound to remind one that this was a country at war. And then my stewardess deposited my lunch tray in front of me. As I reached avidly to attack my butter pat, there, neatly*

*inscribed on it, was the injunction, "*Remember Pearl Harbor.*" It needed the butter to remind one of the guns.*

Detroiters adjusted to wartime austerity without really missing a beat. The November 1942 journal entry of a young housewife expressed the general attitude:

Gas ration to be cut to three gallons a week—coffee sales to be stopped for one week, starting next Sunday, and then rationed to one pound every five weeks—further cut in oil for heating is likely...[M]*eat rationing to start early in new year—few vegetables to be shipped and fewer still to be canned—no raisins or chocolate or olive oil or bacon—less of everything.*

But more of neighborliness and family loyalties and appreciation for the beauty and freedom and worth of the country we have so long taken for granted. We're all in it together and we'll all come out of it with colors flying—no matter how hard and long the way.

"HI-YO SILVER!"

Wartime children were in for stern lectures if they didn't clean their plates, and even the youngest in the family were expected to do their part for the general welfare. But people who grew up during those years tend to recall them more for their excitement than for their deprivations and anxieties.

It was an adventure when the family slept out on the porch on hot nights, in that age before air conditioning. On the way to school, youngsters swapped trading cards featuring silhouettes of enemy planes and kept their eyes raised to sound the alarm in case any of them actually appeared on the horizon. On recess playgrounds, they staged firefights, parachute drops and beach landings. The challenge was deciding who, that day, had to be the Nazis or the banzai-charging Japanese, bound for certain, crushing defeat.

Rules of discipline were often relaxed. Kids stayed outside "until the streetlights came on" (those that were in operation in that time of blackouts), which in summer was after 9:00 p.m. Neighbors kept an eye out for misbehavior, and parents didn't worry when their children made the rounds of the city on their bicycles.

Newspaper "funnies"—black and white through the week, color on Sundays—were a joyful diversion for Detroiters of all ages during World War II. The most popular strips offered simple escape: the domestic misadventures of *Dagwood and Blondie*, the folksy satire of *Li'l Abner*, the romance of *Prince Valiant*. But the demands of civic responsibility intruded even into this realm. Terry and the Pirates battled fascist double-agents, and

Joe Palooka's army buddies "made fluent statements against race prejudice and Anglophobia," according to John Morton Blum.

Comic book sales soared during the war. Soldiers used them to banish the tedium that went with life in uniform—on trains, at bus terminals, in the barracks and out in the field. Deserving of special mention here are two characters custom-built for the times. William Moulton Marsten's Wonder Woman debuted in December 1941, and from the start she gave the enemy fits with her speed, strength and cunning. In her free time, Diana Prince dated the all-American fighter pilot Steve Trevor. The qualities that made the Amazon Warrior so formidable were, not accidently, exactly those attributed to Rosie the Riveter.

Timely Comics' Captain America was the most popular of the war era's superheroes. The story of the ninety-eight-pound weakling who transformed himself into a champion of justice paralleled in many minds the trajectory of the United States. Cap's red, white and blue shield and his homilies about patriotism and teamwork would have been laughable in more sedate times, but they were perfect for this moment in history. The cover of the first issue showed him executing a roundhouse sock to the jaw of Adolf Hitler—not exactly subtle, but satisfying. Later issues continued the theme, serving as a kind of unofficial propaganda for the war effort.

Comic book fans of those years remember the ads they contained for the Johnson Smith Company, a Detroit-based novelty-goods concern that reached a nationwide market. Youngsters sent in their spending money for its joy-buzzers, sneezing powder and "X-ray" specs, only to discover that the fun was more in the anticipation than in the delivery.

Then there was radio. On weekdays, mother listened to *her* programs— soap operas, game shows, the *Camel Comedy Caravan*—until the children came home from school to enjoy *their* favorites. These were mostly superhero serials and cowboy yarns, served up in bite-sized installments of fifteen or thirty minutes—just the thing to revive minds worn down by a day of arithmetic drills and spelling tests.

After dinner, it was time for another round in front of the compact Emerson or the more deluxe Philco set. Youngsters stretched out on the floor as everyone in the family gave their ears and their imaginations over to the variety of fare presented: *Information Please*, *Fibber McGee & Molly*, *Gang Busters* and horror and suspense gems like *Inner Sanctum*, introduced each week by the hair-raising sound of a creaking door. There was also *The Lone Ranger* and *The Green Hornet*, action and adventure shows produced by WXYZ in the Maccabees Building in midtown Detroit.

Syndicated on hundreds of stations across the country, *The Lone Ranger* might have been the most beloved of all programs during the golden age of radio, boasting an average audience of fifteen million—two-thirds of them adults. Sponsored locally by Silvercup Bread, its stirring *William Tell* Overture could be heard from the windows of almost every home in town on Monday, Wednesday and Friday evenings: "Out of the West comes a fiery horse with the speed of light, a cloud of dust, and a hearty *Hi-Yo Silver!*—The Lone Ranger rides again!"

The magic words invited listeners into a world where good always triumphed and a gentleman did not need to resort to his silver bullets to make sure that it did. If only life beyond the darkness of the living room was that simple. Bulletins about the latest Nazi or Japanese atrocities were jarring reminders that it wasn't.

Schoolchildren were exposed with unusual intensity to ideals of civic duty during World War II. They memorized and recited the Gettysburg Address and wrote essays on the Four Freedoms, the best of which were entered into nationwide competitions. At home, they were expected to do their chores and to make sacrifices, just like the adults. A portion of the nickels and dimes they earned ushering or setting pins at the bowling alley was to be earmarked for the purchase of war bonds and stamps.

The rest was squirreled away toward a "big-ticket" item, maybe a used bike, or was spent on small indulgences like an ice cream confection at Cunningham's. The flavors and combinations were the same as ever, but they had new names tailored to wartime: the "Blackout Sundae," the "Paratrooper Shake," the "Flying Fortress" malted.

On Saturday mornings, children were out in force scavenging junk piles and knocking on doors in search of items to stack atop their wagons. Among the most prized were rusted-out tools and lawn mowers, tin cans and wire, rubber bands and string. Movie tickets or a trip to a Tigers game awaited those who accumulated the most booty.

Child care was a chronic challenge for working parents during the war, and Rosies drew particular criticism for their supposed derelictions of duty. They improvised solutions week to week, recruiting older siblings, grandparents and next-door neighbors to help with the baby-sitting. At Willow Run and other defense plants, mothers pooled their resources so they could put in the long hours demanded by their jobs.

Still, youngsters had an unprecedented amount of time away from adult supervision, and of necessity, they grew up fast. This raised concern in some quarters about a rising epidemic of "juvenile delinquency." Newspaper and magazine editors played the issue for its shock value, portraying a vast underworld of neglected youth run amok, populated by hoodlums and fallen teenage daughters—one of them perhaps *yours*—who frequented establishments with pinball machines, dice games and alcohol.

Dubbed V-Girls, the young women afflicted with this pathology were easy to spot in their tight sweaters and short skirts, loitering in front of movie theaters, bus depots and the gates of the local military base as their parents, seduced by inflated wages, were off working the third shift. "It's not enough to sit at home and tap your feet when the tempo starts to quicken," a *Free Press* exposé scolded readers in April 1943. "War is driving men into the Army, women into the plants and the kids into the streets."

In truth, the delinquency scare was overblown, and most of the ink devoted to it amounted to an appeal to the public's taste for the lurid and sensational. Most young people did not run wild during World War II. To the contrary, they demonstrated an admirable maturity in the face of its pressures, and the family unit as a source of structure and discipline suffered no irreparable damage.

During the summer, Detroiters young and old enjoyed day-long excursions to one of the area's several amusement parks. Like the city's movie theaters, Edgewater on the west side and Bob-lo Island downriver boasted record attendance during the war years.

The famous Bob-lo boats stayed in operation despite the shortage of personnel qualified to pilot them, who were mostly away in the navy or the merchant marine. Race segregation rules applied, but children gave such matters little thought as they rode the wooden roller coasters or got soaked splashing through the Tunnel of Love. At night, couples enjoyed the island's open-air dance pavilion, and spots on the ferries' romantic moonlight cruises were always in high demand.

Bob-lo's lone concession to the war was the scuttling of its run from Amherstberg on the Canadian side in 1940. The change came after a member of the Bund was intercepted trying to slip into the United States through its lax customs checkpoint.

"HITTING ONE AGAINST HITLER"

Sports were another reliable diversion from the war. Through radio, newsreel and newspaper accounts, fans around the country followed heavyweight champion Joe Louis, who, as we have seen, suspended his boxing career to go into the army as a private. "I don't want any favors," declared the twenty-seven-year-old Detroit native at his induction ceremony.

The War Department understood that the Brown Bomber's greatest value was in the ring, and over the next three years Louis traveled seventy thousand miles visiting hospitals, signing autographs and staging exhibitions to raise money for charity. An estimated five million men got to see the champ in person, and at his insistence, the crowds who came to watch him were always integrated.

Known for his soft-spoken humility (not to mention a deadly, lightning-fast right hand), Louis won over Americans of all backgrounds with his blitzkrieg-like demolition of the German fighter Max Schmeling in 1938. Now he was another kind of icon, a model of righteous power just when the country needed it. "Maybe my next fight will be against Max in no-man's land," Joe quipped to reporters. "I won't be pulling any punches."

Though the quality of play was compromised, intercollegiate sports continued during World War II. "This year we will play seventeen-year-old basketball," the athletic director at the University of Detroit said on the eve of the 1943 campaign. "Not a single member of last year's team is returning, varsity or reserve." The Titans managed a 12-6 record that year, against similarly diluted competition.

Pro sports were affected by the talent drain, too. With an assortment of lumbering, butter-fingered players, the no-name Detroit Lions gamely hosted an abbreviated schedule each fall at Briggs Stadium. The going was rough for fans of the Honolulu blue and silver—the team went winless in 1942—but people kept coming out, in all kinds of weather, to lend their support.

At Olympia Stadium, the Red Wings also carried on, their contests always an event in hockey-mad Detroit. And the Wings gave fans something to think about besides war headlines, defeating the Boston Bruins in the 1943 NHL finals to earn their third Stanley Cup. Players wore a large "V" emblem on their red-and-white jerseys, underscored by three dots and a dash—Morse code for, again, "V" for "Victory." Next to it was a circular patch reminding patrons to tithe 10 percent of their pay for war bonds, conveniently on sale at a booth near the concession stand.

Lineups for the wartime Wings were ever-changing, and plenty of "too-young" and "too-old" players got a chance to skate the choppy Olympia ice. In all, twenty-four regulars were off in the service, including stalwarts Sid Abel, Harry Watson and Jack Stewart.

Fans had little reason to notice Joe Turner, a baby-faced goalie prospect from Windsor who ended up playing but a single game for the Detroit Red Wings. Joe had the potential to become one of the greats, the scouts agreed, but he decided after the '42 season to hang up his skates and volunteer for U.S. Army. There were, he told friends and family, more important things to attend to than hockey.

On December 13, 1944, while fighting with his infantry unit in the Hurtgen Forest in Germany, Lieutenant Turner went missing. Within days came confirmation that he had been killed in action. He was twenty-three.

There were countless Joe Turners in the Second World War, men cut down before their prime, leaving only memories and the appalling tragedy of unfulfilled promise. Along with our nostalgia for swing music and bobby-soxers, the nearness of death everyone sensed during those years should never be forgotten. "The class just ahead of me in college was virtually wiped out," writer William Stryon observed, reminding us of the stark truth. "Beautiful fellows who had won basketball championships and Phi Beta Kappa keys died like ants in the Normandy invasion."

Baseball was the favorite sport of African Americans in 1940s Detroit, and they played it in streets and alleys and on muddy park diamonds throughout the city. Despite the strong interest, there was no local Negro League franchise during the war years. Joe Louis flirted with investing in a team but decided instead to support pro softball. The Brown Bombers were the subject of many a barbershop conversation, and by all accounts the majority owner played a creditable first base for his team before going into the army. The Detroit Giants, a member of the short-lived Negro Major Leagues, performed in front of crowds as large as five thousand in 1942.

Visits by the barnstorming Kansas City Monarchs were much-anticipated occasions for Detroit baseball fans of all colors, offering them a chance to see in the flesh the likes of Satchel Paige, Josh Gibson and Buck Williams—players as good as or better than any in the white major leagues. Forty thousand turned out at Briggs for one Monarchs exhibition. Their excellence and flash was a particular source of pride for African Americans, and patrons in the stands dressed accordingly—the men in fedoras and crisp suits and ties, the women decked out in their Sunday best with gloves and colorful hats.

One of baseball's storied franchises, the Detroit Tigers played their games uninterrupted through World War II. This was in the spirit of President Roosevelt's statement that the national pastime was too important to morale to be suspended. The Tigers enjoyed "the most loyal following of any team in the major leagues," according to the 1940 WPA *Guide to Michigan*. "The three daily newspapers carry column after column of baseball news, not simply in the sport sections, but in front page streamer headlines when a momentous event occurs, such as Hank Greenberg's spraining his wrist."

With his towering home runs, the six-four "Hammerin' Hank" was Detroit's answer to Babe Ruth, striking terror into the hearts of pitchers all around the majors over the course of his career. Greenberg led his team to a World Series championship in 1935 and was twice voted the American League's Most Valuable Player. He was admired by teammates and opponents alike for his unwavering professionalism and sportsmanship, on and off the field.

Hank was a folk hero to all Tiger fans, but he had special importance for members of Detroit's Jewish community. Born Hyman Greenberg in the Bronx to Orthodox parents from Romania, he grew up celebrating his faith without self-consciousness or apology. He continued the practice as a big-leaguer, declining to take the field on Yom Kippur and other high holidays. This was a bold statement in the Detroit of Henry Ford and Father Coughlin, local figures notorious for their anti-Semitic pronouncements.

Greenberg was in demand as a speaker at temples, schools and community centers and as a dinner guest in the homes of prominent Jewish families. While he never courted the role as champion of his faith, Hank came to accept it as a responsibility that went with his celebrity—against the backdrop of burning synagogues and smashed shop windows in Germany.

Like Joe Louis, who felt the weight of an entire race on his shoulders every time he stepped into the boxing ring, so did Hank Greenberg face pressures that went far beyond his sport. He handled himself with dignity, letting his bat and glove do the talking and doing his best to ignore the slurs and provocations that came his way all the time in every ballpark. "I was always in the spotlight," Greenberg said later. "I was there every day, and if I had a bad day, every son-of-a-bitch was calling me names. I had to make good. I came to feel that if I, a Jew, hit a home run, I was hitting one against Hitler."

Detroit made it back to the World Series in 1940 but lost to Cincinnati. By spring training the next year, many of the team's established players had departed for military duty, including its slugging superstar. Like Joe Louis, "Hammerin' Hank" took a big pay cut when he joined the army—from an annual salary of $50,000, tops in the majors, to $21 a month. Discharged

Sports heavyweights Hank Greenberg and Joe Louis share a light moment at Briggs Stadium. Both men served in the military during World War II. *Courtesy Reuther Archives.*

briefly in 1941, he went back in as a member of the air corps right after Pearl Harbor.

Greenberg brushed off questions about his sacrifice. "We are in trouble," he explained to a reporter, "and there is only one thing for me to do—return to the service. This doubtless means I am finished with baseball and it would be silly of me to say I do not leave it without a pang. But all of us are confronted with a terrible task—the defense of our country and the fight for our lives."

Six months before the Japanese attack—in the middle of that last glorious peacetime summer of 1941—Briggs Stadium played host to an especially dramatic All-Star Game. Tiger loyalists cheered wildly when Boston's Ted Williams, on his way to a .400 season (and then service as a marine fighter pilot), blasted a ninth-inning homer to lead the American League over the Nationals, 7–5.

"The Corner" at Michigan and Trumbull was a changed place once the country went to war—and not always in a good way. The box office sagged, and players complained about the "dead" ball they were being asked to hit, made of inferior materials due to the shortage of cork and rubber. Just as bad in the view of many fans, the Goebels and Strohs they guzzled on hot days were a diluted "3.2" mixture.

Play-by-play announcers were instructed not to mention weather conditions during broadcasts, for fear that unfriendly ears might be listening. The commissioner's office ordered all teams to post instructions on the back of stadium seats, telling patrons what to do in the event of an enemy attack. The main thing was to stay calm. "Should an air raid siren sound while you're watching the game, don't leave the ballpark," the notices read. "You'll probably be sitting in the best bomb shelter in the neighborhood."

Radio and print journalists alike were also asked to tone down the hyperbole usually associated with sports. The Associated Press circulated a memo to its correspondents on the baseball beat, reminding them to keep the games they covered in perspective: "There should be a ban on flowery, overenthusiastic, lyrical sports writing for the duration. Remembering the exploits of military heroes, it does not seem appropriate to overdo the use of such words as 'courageous,' 'gallant,' 'fighting.' It doesn't take much 'courage' to overcome a two-run lead in the ninth."

The play on the field was as watered down as the beer. Given the team's patchwork design, this was to be expected, but that did not make it any easier to watch. Like the Yankees without DiMaggio and the Bosox without

Williams, the Tigers without Greenberg were, as one reporter indelicately put it, "a motley collection of teenagers, has-beens, and selective service rejects." A sportswriter for *Time* spoke of big-league rosters "as full of unknown names as Y.M.C.A. hotel registers."

And yet FDR was right: baseball was integral to community spirit, and it had to go on. Detroiters looked past the on-field ineptitude and made the best of what they had. For at least a few moments at every game, the energy at Briggs crackled with patriotic feeling. Men and women in uniform and patrons who brought in scrap donations were admitted at a discount. Then it was time for "The Star-Spangled Banner," adopted league-wide during the war as part of the pregame ritual. Hats were removed and hands went to hearts as the crowd rose as one to its feet. And the singing of the anthem in those days was no spectator sport—*everyone* joined in, for a reading that made up in sincerity what it lacked in artistic quality.

The war insinuated itself into every aspect of the fans' experience. There were, of course, the ubiquitous war bond booths and posters reminding everyone of how privileged they were to be able to drowse in the sun-warmed bleachers on a weekday afternoon. Patrons gave foul balls to stadium officials, knowing that, however scuffed and marked-up, they would be shipped to soldiers in North Africa or on a remote island in the Pacific, where men looked to a children's game for a taste of home.

Things were looking up for the Tigers in the summer of '45. Led by Dizzy Trout and Hal Newhouser—the latter arguably the most dominant pitcher in the majors during the war—they won more games than they lost, for the first time in years. Newhouser had tried to enlist in the service but was rejected due to a heart defect. The problem didn't seem to affect his work on the mound.

Meanwhile, players with familiar names, men who had sacrificed their most productive athletic years to serve their country, were coming back, raising the level of play and the hopes of fans in a number of big-league cities. Attendance at Briggs was up as the Tigers found themselves in a pennant race. Even those who were not ordinarily baseball fans began to check the sports page every day.

PART IV
VICTORY!

Wartime life was never looked on as a way of life; it was an interlude.

—Richard Lingeman

A WAR "HALF-WON"

Symbols matter in war, and there was no better symbol of the Motor City's grit and determination—its moxie, to use a word then in popular use—than the USS *Detroit*, the light navy cruiser that was its namesake. Civilians took heart as they tracked its fortunes in the newspapers and on newsreels.

The *Detroit* was in the middle of it all when the war started that Sunday morning in Hawaii. The crew managed to guide it to open water and got off some rounds of antiaircraft fire, downing a couple of enemy torpedo planes. During the war, the ship performed escort duties in the dangerous seas off the Aleutians.

The *Detroit* was there, too, for the war's final chapter on September 2, 1945. Battered but still afloat, it stood anchored in Tokyo Harbor as the ceremony marking the official end of hostilities was conducted on the deck of the *Missouri*. A long, winding circle was now closed.

When the first reports of the Japanese surrender had broken a couple of weeks earlier, half a million Detroiters rushed into the streets to celebrate. Revelers bathed in the fountain at Grand Circus Park, the city's Times Square. Surging up and down the length of Woodward Avenue, they laughed, cried and shouted with abandon. The same atmosphere prevailed in the neighborhoods and suburbs. "PEACE! PEACE! PEACE!" exulted the *Free Press* the next morning. "City Greets End with Wildest Day."

It had been a roller-coaster year.

First there was the death of President Roosevelt on April 12 at his retreat in Warm Springs, Georgia, an event that struck most Americans, whether at home or on some far-flung battle front, like "a physical blow," in the words of his friend Winston Churchill. FDR's larger-than-life persona obscured the fact that he had been ailing for some time, and his abrupt passing caught almost everyone by surprise.

Free Press staffer Harry Fenton was standing next to the office teletype machine when the message came across late that afternoon, a little before 6:00 p.m. "Suddenly, the flash bell began to ring," a man who interviewed him later wrote. "Conversation in the newsroom ceased; many thought the bells might presage the end of the war. Fenton, the wire copy in his hands and tears in his eyes, told the others: Roosevelt is dead."

After a few seconds of stunned silence, people began to channel their grief into the job of getting extra editions out onto the street.

Fate cheated the president from seeing his labors through to their completion. At the family's request, newspapers across the country listed "Roosevelt, Franklin Delano" as simply one name on an alphabetical list of the war dead for the day, accompanied by the spare designation of rank, "Commander-in-Chief." It was a gesture in perfect keeping with the democratic values he had so valiantly championed.

Barbara Williams remembered that her parents "worshipped" FDR, who had been a rock for them over a dozen storm-tossed years. His passing cast a pall over their house at Six Mile and Wildemere that did not lift for days. Years later, Barbara could re-create in minute detail the scene in the kitchen. There was a phone call, and then her normally stoic mother slumped down on a chair at the dining table, hand at her mouth, face ashen. "Wait till your *father* hears this," she whispered vacantly, dabbing her eyes and shaking her head in disbelief.

It was a death in the family. By evening, front porches all along Barbara's street were filled with men pacing and smoking as they speculated about "Harry Truman," the new man in charge—up to then, hardly a household name. On the day of the state funeral, schools, theaters and even saloons were locked and empty. At precisely 4:00 p.m., as the broadcast service commenced in Washington, everything stopped. The next weekend, it was hard to find a seat in churches and synagogues.

Less than a month later, on May 8, came word of the German surrender and the raucous excitement of V-E Day. But that good news was tempered by the business still to be finished with Japan. It would be a long summer ahead for those with loved ones stationed in the Pacific or on their way there from Europe.

The atomic bomb—whatever *that* was—bought reprieve from the invasion that had for so long seemed a bloody inevitability. Few at the time questioned

Truman's decision to use the doomsday weapon. It was just revenge for December 7, it pacified an implacable enemy and, in the end, it spared lives on *both* sides. Husbands, boyfriends and sons would be coming home soon.

Detroiters were as much in the dark as other Americans about what had been unleashed in their name on Hiroshima and Nagasaki, but they were already accustomed to the end-of-the-world destruction wrought by conventional bombs. The front page of the August 2 *Free Press* featured this banner headline, applauded heartily by its war-weary readers: "800 B-29S ROCK JAP CITIES IN HISTORY'S BIGGEST RAID."

To be sure, the announcement of the first nuclear attack prompted some head-scratching and misgivings about what it meant for the future. "ATOMS SMASH JAPAN," the *Free Press* reported on August 7. "Terrible Bomb Heralds New Era."

But alongside this narrative was a campaign to reassure people that this new energy source would be domesticated. A feature story in the *Detroit News* offered readers the vision of a better, more bountiful future in which "automobiles, trains and airplanes [will] run for a lifetime on a bit of stuff from which atomic power can be released at will." Soon there would be "furnaces of vest-pocket size" and ocean liners circumnavigating the planet without refueling.

Concerns about radioactivity, waste disposal and other safety problems were brushed aside. Surely the ingenuity that had created the bomb would find ways to negate the dangers that came with it. "The potential of the atomic age is limited only by the bounds of man's imagination," the *News* concluded, with perhaps a forced grandiosity. "No speculation could be too fantastic."

Nuclear fallout and perpetual-motion machines were distant concerns for most Americans in that first blush of victory, however. There was too much pent-up *human* energy to blow off to bother fretting about the long run. As

Most Detroiters reacted to the A-bomb with relief. *Courtesy Michael Hauser.*

129

night fell on V-J Day, August 14, 1945, pandemonium reigned in cities and towns across the nation. Horns honked, sirens blared and firecrackers and cherry bombs exploded. Bar patrons sparred to buy the next round. Perfect strangers embraced and kissed on the street.

Fifteen-year-old Barbara Williams wanted to head downtown "to kiss a sailor"—*any* sailor would do. Her father had other ideas, however, and a last-minute babysitting job materialized to derail her plans, to her everlasting chagrin.

Grandparents tossed back shots of whiskey and danced and reeled as they had not done in years. Heavy-lidded children in pajamas were allowed to stay up to witness the once-in-a-lifetime revelry. The adults were so giddy that even the youngest must have sensed that something very big and very good had happened.

The scene was repeated from Hamtramck to the *barrio* in southwest Detroit, from Dearborn's Middle Eastern enclave to Chinatown and Paradise Valley. The party continued through the night in Wyandotte,

"City's Wildest Day," August 14, 1945. *Courtesy Reuther Archives.*

Revelers celebrating the end of the war. *Courtesy Reuther Archives.*

Ferndale, Royal Oak, Warren and St. Clair Shores. A lot of coupon books went into the trash, even though rationing was still in effect. Lines snaked around gas stations and grocery stores as customers demanded what they wanted, without restraint, for the first time in memory. Besieged proprietors bent the rules to accommodate them.

By the time the sun rose the next day, work crews were already fanning out across the city to clean up the mess. Those nursing hangovers struggled even to get out of bed. Bells tolled in churches, and the one atop the University of Detroit clock tower sounded 137 times in tribute to the students who would not be coming back in the fall. It was an invitation to reflect on the reasons all those young lives had been sacrificed.

At a ceremony in front of city hall that afternoon, a parade of dignitaries stepped to the microphone to offer their answers. The most eloquent was Frank Murphy, Detroit's former mayor and now a member of the U.S. Supreme Court. Murphy had distinguished himself with a dissent in the *Korematsu* case, in which he argued that the internment of Japanese Americans violated their constitutional rights.

Thinking of the Sojourner Truth and Belle Isle riots—traumas many Detroiters would just as soon have expunged from their memories—Justice

Above: V-J Day in Detroit's Chinatown. *Courtesy Reuther Archives.*

Left: University of Detroit clock tower. Dedicated to honor the dead of the First World War, its bell tolled 137 times in memory of those lost in the Second. *Courtesy University of Detroit Mercy Library.*

Murphy challenged the crowd to fight injustice at home with the same vigor that they had brought to the battle against adversaries overseas. "Unless we cleanse our hearts of hate—racial and religious," he warned, "this war will only be half-won." The sermon drew robust applause.

A letter to *Time* that week from a serviceman stationed in Florida echoed the idea that the passions let loose by the war would not be so easily put back on the shelf. "Why stop at just hating Japs?" the army lieutenant demanded, with mock earnestness.

> *Thousands of our boys will come home from the Western Front hating the Germans.* [T]*hese men* [could get] *together with all the whites who hate the Negroes, the gentiles who hate the Jews, the Southerners who hate the Yankees, the Northerners who hate the Miamians, the isolationists who hate the British, the Texans who hate the "spicks," the Protestants who hate the "micks," the Kentuckians who hate the "revenooers,"* ad infinitum.

In contrast to the ravaged landscapes of Europe and Asia, Detroit and other American cities emerged from the Second World War essentially unscathed. The air raid drills, blackout curtains and "refuge rooms" turned out not to be unnecessary—the Motor City was simply too far beyond the range of even the most sophisticated Axis bombers to have ever been in serious danger. Rumors of gun-toting enemy agents proved false every time, and the Nazi U-boats prowling the Great Lakes turned out to be figments of a few excitable imaginations.

There is an exception to this picture of safety, however, a bizarre footnote to the concluding phase of America's war in the Pacific largely forgotten today. Even with their naval and air forces obliterated and a civilian population on the edge of starvation, Hirohito's generals refused to accept defeat, and in the fall and winter of 1944–45 they authorized the launch of what one historian has called "the first weapons of intercontinental warfare." Waves of bomb-carrying paper balloons thirty feet in diameter were released into the air from selected sites in Japan, with the hope that high-altitude winds would carry them over the ocean and onto the American mainland. Perhaps they would sow come kind of panic, and the enemy's morale would be shaken.

Only a fraction of the nine thousand *fu-go* ("wind-ship weapon") devices made it across. In all, three hundred or so were either spotted or recovered at random locations in the United States, mostly in the western states. They sparked a few forest fires, and one even produced casualties, killing six people in Oregon unlucky enough to have been camping near the spot where it touched down and, on a delayed fuse, detonated.

Incredibly, one of the "Fire Balloons" drifted as far east as Michigan, a lone, towering *War of the Worlds*–type UFO that settled down harmlessly in a vegetable garden just outside the rural hamlet of Farmington, northwest of Detroit. The man who unearthed the odd "tin can" with his shovel showed it to his neighbor, a police officer, and soon experts from Washington confirmed that it was an incendiary device of Japanese origin.

The details of the Michigan balloon bomb were withheld from the public. But no damage was done; no army base, air field or munitions plant was disrupted, even for a second. However ingenious in concept, Tokyo's *fu-go* assault was a last-ditch act of desperation doomed to failure.

"RECONVERSION"

By the summer of 1945, GIs in large numbers were returning home on ships and troop trains, eager to collect their discharge benefits and resume the comforts of civilian life. There were tearful reunions at Michigan Central and other rail and bus stations as families turned out to receive their warriors, some of whom had been gone four years or more. Some men laid eyes on their young children (the so-called goodbye babies) for the first time.

There followed a period of adjustment for everyone, more or less rocky. Women were asked to surrender their hard-won independence, while the ex-GIs exchanged the structure and camaraderie that had gotten them through the war for a peacetime world of complexity and choices. They were expected to cut back on swearing and drinking, sleep at night in a proper bed and shave first thing every morning.

The challenge of return was a popular subject for Hollywood films just after the war. The Oscar-winning *Best Years of Our Lives* (1946) is a time capsule of that moment, telling with unusual sensitivity the story of three physically and psychologically wounded veterans and the families who try to comfort and understand them. As on the screen, many ex-soldiers came back to "war brides" they barely knew, with predictably mixed results. In our nostalgia, it is easy to forget that there were as many *divorces* when the boys came home as weddings.

Sooner or later, the vets were ready to reclaim their places in the workforce. Many employers had reserved positions for them, and in union shops, soldiers got seniority credit for their time in the service. It was a combination women new to the workforce could not hope to match. Despite her contributions to victory, Rosie was asked to set down the rivet bucket and abandon her bridgehead into the "man's world" of high-wage labor. This despite a *Wall Street Journal* survey showing that three in four wanted to keep their jobs.

Betty Oelke recalled her feelings of emptiness and loss after she and her husband left Willow Run and returned to their small town in rural Michigan. "I'd been around people all of the time," she explained, "and when we moved to Milan I was alone all the time. Once you work, you want to keep on doing it. I missed the people and all of the noise and I wished I was back. I felt quite proud working in the bomber plant. Most of us did."

Many Rosies were happy to embrace marriage, motherhood and the traditional responsibilities of family life. They were encouraged in this (some might say "brainwashed") by the women's magazines of the day, where the message changed overnight to suit new priorities. "The Kitchen—Women's Big Post-War Goal," read one feature. Preparation time for recipes doubled and trebled, aprons replaced dungarees, snoods and bandanas. Madison Avenue pushed images of housewives in ecstasy over the latest-model washing machine or vacuum cleaner.

The shift in the movies was equally abrupt. "The independent women earlier portrayed by Katherine Hepburn and Joan Crawford disappeared from the screen, and were supplanted by Doris Day and Donna Reed as the wholesome girl next door," Sherna Berger Gluck has observed. The cinematic alternative to domesticity was the sex goddess. It is worth noting that "Marilyn Monroe" worked in a California aircraft plant during the war, when she was still Norma Jean Baker.

Other unemployed Rosies had to get by in the low-wage, low-status economy still open to women. Some beat the odds and established successful careers outside the home. After getting her pink slip from The Run, single parent Rose Monroe supported her two children by driving a cab and operating a beauty salon. In time, she saved enough to invest in a construction business, which thrived in the postwar housing boom.

Detroit's returning veterans took advantage of the GI Bill to attend day and evening classes at local trade schools and universities—an opportunity their parents would never have dreamt possible. Between 1944 and 1946, enrollment at the University of Detroit soared from 1,821 to 7,489. Most of the incoming freshmen were in their mid-twenties or older and just out of the service.

Professors at the U of D and Wayne State would recall with fondness the crowded classrooms of the postwar years. It was invigorating to engage with young men so willing to challenge received ideas and so determined to measure them against their own rich experiences. The Allen Park or Grosse Pointe lad back from action against Panzer divisions or dive-bombing Zeroes had opinions about the world, and he was not afraid to express them.

Things could get off-color, even in the groves of academe. In their German classes, ex-POWs introduced words and phrases not found in the textbook. And a U of D legend tells of the elderly Jesuit priest who asked his engineering student to cover strategic places on his bomber jacket with masking tape, to conceal pin-up anatomical references unfit for view on campus. It was a reasonable request, and the ex-pilot complied without complaint.

Production in Detroit's defense plants began to ease even before the Axis had been completely vanquished, and by 1945 there was talk of a new danger on the homefront: apathy. Radio and newspaper commentators held forth on the contagion of "victory-itis." "DON'T STOP BUYING…THEY'RE STILL DYING!" admonished war bond posters at the movie theaters.

In July 1945, a full-page ad in *Time* for Pepsodent toothpaste warned readers to be wary of neighbors and coworkers who had taken their eyes off the ball and become "Optimistic Olivers."

These Men Are Dangerous Citizens.

[T]*hey're worth a million dollars to our enemies. This "it-won't-be-long-now" talk spreads like wildfire. Rosie the Riveter and her coworkers take an afternoon off for a permanent…Mrs. Jones isn't so careful about saving her tin cans…Joe Zilch guesses he doesn't have to put so much of his paycheck into War Bonds…There's no shortcut to victory. It's a long road—an expensive trip!*

The anti-apathy campaign worked: bond sales actually increased in the last months of the war.

Geopolitics were changing fast, and attitudes lagged in catching up. American business continued to praise Red Army troops for their courage and trumpet the value of the lend-lease aid sent to help them even as the shotgun marriage between the United States and the Soviet Union was coming apart. A May 1945 ad for Studebaker highlighted the role its "deuce-and-a-half" trucks had played in driving back the *Wehrmacht* on the Eastern Front. A group of Russian officers, it noted with pride, sent the company and its employees a commemorative photo album as a token of their gratitude. G.I. Joe and Ivan still wanted to be friends, but the iron curtain was about to come down on this kind of brotherly affection. Soon there would be no more references in the American press to Marshall Stalin as kindly, misunderstood "Uncle Joe."

Like munitions plants everywhere, Willow Run phased down operations as the need for its products waned. No one should have been surprised by this. Even The Run's most ardent champion, Edsel Ford, knew from the start that his bomber factory would be a temporary thing—"as expendable as a battleship," he said just before his death.

This reflected a more general attitude among Americans, one not limited to issues of production. As Richard Lingeman has concluded, for most people, "wartime life was never looked upon as a way of life; it was an interlude."

The last of Willow Run's 8,685 Liberators rolled off the line on June 25, 1945, its nose section bearing the logo "HENRY FORD." In a magnanimous gesture his son would have appreciated, the elderly Mr. Ford ordered its removal so that the men and women who built the plane could make their own inscriptions. Hundreds stood in line to accept the invitation.

Similar rituals took place at Ford's Rouge, the Packard plant and Chrysler's Warren Arsenal complex, where an astonishing 22,234 tanks had been manufactured in less than four years. The nation wasted little time in beating its swords into ploughshares, and all kinds of ordnance was relegated, without hesitation or sentimentality, to the junkyard. By the fall of 1945, hundreds of B-24s were sitting idle in neat rows at airfields, classified as "war surplus" to be disassembled and recycled. After two decades of faithful service, the USS *Detroit* was decommissioned and sold for scrap in February 1946.

Even Captain America, the comic book embodiment of the nation's fighting spirit, found himself suddenly expendable once the reason for his existence was over. Cap's sales went into decline, and in 1950 he was consigned to limbo, entombed by his creators in a prison of ice. There he would remain until Hollywood resuscitated him for a series of digitally enhanced big-screen blockbusters in the twenty-first century. Their global box office success is evidence that a market for simple, nostalgic heroes endures.

With two million residents, Detroit ranked as the fourth-largest city in the United States in 1950. The census numbers were deceiving, however—forces were already well in motion that would reverse the wartime population surge. Peace brought with it a construction boom, but the new office complexes and manufacturing plants were built on cheap land outside the city limits. And enterprising developers grasped the opportunities that were opening up as veterans and their brides got to work on a baby boom. Using methods pioneered by the Seabees to build instant air bases in the Pacific, they rushed to break ground for the Levittown-style "pre-fab" housing tracts that would sap so much of the vitality of urban centers around the country in the years to come.

With the (mostly white) flight of families to the suburbs came shopping centers like Northland on Eight Mile, anchored by satellites of Hudson's and the other big downtown department stores. Why fight the crowds in the city when there were so many options close at hand, with free parking to boot? The malls, in turn, brought other now-familiar elements of car culture with them—fast-food and drugstore chains, big-box hardware emporiums and family entertainment venues like the Ford-Wyoming Drive-In in Dearborn.

Millions in other parts of the world struggled for bare survival in the war's immediate aftermath. "HUNGRY EUROPE FACES A BLEAK, HEATLESS WINTER," the *Free Press* reported in late September 1945. But for Americans, a cornucopia beckoned. Aching to shake off years of austerity, they went on a spending spree, purchasing air-conditioners, frost-free refrigerators and myriad other consumer goods. Soon, they would be buying televisions.

The exodus to the suburbs was, in part, an unintended consequence of the ease of movement made possible by Detroit's wartime freeways. Bulldozed to make way for I-375 as part of an "urban renewal" plan that spelled doom for working-class neighborhoods throughout the city, Paradise Valley exists now only in memory. In their rush to sweep away the old, advocates of "progress" showed precious little concern for the human costs inflicted, the damage done to community and sense of place.

Historical marker for Paradise Valley, the main street of wartime Detroit's black culture. *Courtesy ReShawn Wilder.*

Detroit's automakers managed a relatively smooth transition back to passenger cars. People wanting to junk their weathered jalopies descended on showrooms in record numbers. To meet the demand, some of the first postwar models were hurried off the line with wooden bumpers. Magazine ads cultivated the appetite, like the one that counseled soldiers' families on "the things they will find nice to come home to." Among these were "such pleasures as an open road, a glorious day—and a bright and lively Buick."

Kaiser-Fraser purchased the Willow Run complex in 1946, and what Lindbergh once hailed as "the Grand Canyon of the mechanized world" now had a new mission: satisfying the whims of a fickle, style-conscious buying public. Car sales soared even as the industry consolidated and Kaiser, Hudson, DeSoto and other mid-sized companies bit the dust. The Packard plant was shuttered and padlocked in 1956—the same year, ironically, that Detroit's last streetcar rumbled down the center of Woodward Avenue.

Some GIs left Michigan altogether once they got out of the service. Alixa Naff's brothers traveled widely during the war, and their horizons now went beyond running the family grocery in Highland Park. George, who flew navy fighters, and Nick, an officer in the air transport command, returned to Detroit just long enough to get married and then lit out for California. Alixa and her widowed father soon followed.

REVERBERATIONS

etroit's annual Veterans Day parade on November 11, 1945, was, as might be expected, an unusually poignant event, aimed at comforting families with fresh losses and soldiers coming to terms with wounds of body and mind. An observer in the throng of 150,000 gave this description: "[A]long the route where hundreds of mothers had marched against war on Armistice Day, 1939, now hundreds of Gold Star mothers and disabled ex-GIs sat in places of honor on the reviewing stand. The crowd cheered the marching columns of veterans, especially the service men of the Second World War, their rows of campaign ribbons gleaming."

Reverberations from the war would continue for decades, manifesting in all kinds of ways. In 1949, the Detroit Institute of Art was the first major museum in the country to return to its rightful owner a work looted by the Nazis—Monet's *The Seine at Asnieres*. It happened again in 2002 with *A Man-O-War and Other Ships Off the Dutch Coast*, a seascape by seventeenth-century master Ludolf Backhuysen. Once the legal issues were sorted out, the DIA was permitted to keep the piece on loan in its collections. Other examples of plundered art will no doubt emerge as the detective work goes on.

Over the years, Detroit has dedicated its share of monuments to the service men and women of World War II. They range in scale from the stately Grosse Pointe War Memorial on Lake St. Clair to the somewhat overgrown plaque on the median at Lahser and Outer Drive, dedicated in 1943 by the Brightmoor community. Drivers speed by every day without noticing it.

Monument at Lahser and Outer Drive, in the westside Brightmoor neighborhood (dedicated in 1943). Drivers speed by daily without noticing it. *Courtesy ReShawn Wilder.*

In cemeteries are the final resting places of thousands who fought in the war, headstones indicating the dates and branch of their service. Some made it into old age; others were cut down far too early, suspended forever in our minds as boys of eighteen or twenty. A few fell in the heroic, Audie Murphy–like poses we know so well from the movies, but many more died in the mundane tragedies that are a part of all wars, ancient and modern. The precise circumstances often lie buried with them.

John Knight, owner of the *Detroit Free Press*, offered a eulogy for the dead in his column of April 22, 1945. John Jr., his eldest son, had been killed in Europe the month before, during the final senseless weeks of Nazi resistance. A guarded man by nature, Knight decided to go public with his grief to honor his son's memory and to be a voice for others dealing with the same kind of loss. "Johnny is gone," he began, in a key anguished and bitter. "The lovable kid who never had a vicious thought in his life is sleeping in Germany because of the mad, senseless ambitions of a demented paranoiac; because in the last 20 years the 'statesmen' of Europe have repeatedly sacrificed principle on the altar of power politics."

Knight shared the words of his son's infantry buddy, who had written to him that Johnny "was killed the same way he lived, doing just a little more than anyone asked him to do, giving more than he was required to give."

"The great tragedy of the Johnnys, the Sams, the Petes, the Joes and all the thousands of other fine young men who have died for us is that few of them ever had a real chance at life," Knight lamented. Now the challenge of building a peace worthy of their sacrifice remained. "To the Johnnys who are gone and the millions of Johnnys to come, let it at least be proved by our acts that we sought redemption and endeavored to make atonement for the sins of a shallow, self-indulgent and greedy generation."

Some soldiers died in controversy. Eddie Slovik grew up poor on the streets of Hamtramck, and as a teenager, he had his share of scrapes with the law. Like a lot of kids with a rap sheet, Eddie ended up being drafted, never really understanding what would be expected of him once he got to the war zone.

In October 1944, Private Slovik wandered off from his infantry unit in France as it disintegrated in the face of heavy German shelling. After the MPs picked him up he decided—against the advice of friends and even his commanding officer—to sign a written confession to the crime of desertion. In the chaos of shifting battle lines, plenty of other men had gone AWOL without serious consequences. Besides, he figured, a stretch in the brig, even a long one, was better than a ticket back to the killing fields of the front.

Unfortunately for Slovik, the military authorities decided to make an example out of him, and upon his conviction they ordered the maximum punishment—death by firing squad. The condemned protested his treatment all the way to the end. "They're shooting me," he insisted, "for the bread and chewing-gum I stole when I was 12 years old."

Eddie Slovik, twenty-four years old—coward or scapegoat, depending on your angle of view—was buried without ceremony near the village of Sainte-Marie-aux-Mines, in a corner of a church graveyard reserved for those who had died dishonorably. Decades later, a Polish American veterans group in Hamtramck petitioned for the return of his remains, and in 1987 they were reinterred in Detroit's historic Woodmere Cemetery. To this day, Slovik's headstone attracts history buffs, vandals and graffiti artists.

Beyond plaques, headstones and medal ceremonies, Detroit offers a multitude of less formal monuments evoking the lives lived during the Second World War.

The Tigers no longer play at the "the Corner," of course. A vacant lot is all that remains where Briggs Stadium once stood, and the void haunts visitors who come by to reminisce. But as the property awaits a developer, it has been adopted by an ad hoc group of diehard fans, with the city's cautious approval. On warm-weather Sundays, members of the Navin Field Grounds Crew (a reference to the original stadium on the site) show up to pull weeds, rake debris and mow the grass on the hallowed ground. Spirited pick-up games follow once the chores are done.

Gone, too, is the cracker box Olympia Stadium on Grand River, where the Red Wings won so many Stanley Cups. Its precarious balconies and beer-

and-cigar-smoke atmosphere are long-ago victims of the wrecking ball. But there are still people around who were there during the Old Red Brick Barn's heyday, and they keep its memories alive for their grandchildren. Canada's International Hockey League honored Joe Turner, the promising goalie who lost his life in the last months of the war, by naming its championship trophy after him.

Not far from the Briggs and Olympia sites is the mammoth Michigan Central train station, built solidly enough, it seems, to last forever. Once congested with rail and foot traffic, it stands now empty and brooding, marking time until a suitor comes along to restore its lost grandeur.

Detroit's movie theaters are, sadly, almost all extinct. After a stretch as an art house and then several years vacant, the Telenews on Woodward has been recently reborn as the techno nightclub Bleu. It's a safe bet that the young people who dance there on the weekends know next to nothing about its past.

But lovingly rehabilitated treasures like the Fox downtown and the Redford at Lahser and Six Mile, its Japanese motifs brought back to life by the painstaking efforts of volunteers with the Motor City Theatre Organ Society, still transport those willing to take the ride back to the days when attending a motion picture was an *event*. Children respond with awe to the trappings of these venerable buildings, where once upon a time their great-grandparents spent so many pleasurable hours sitting in the dark.

Redford Theatre marquee, 2015. *Photo by Gregory Sumner.*

The Dakota Rathskeller, still going strong in 2015. *Courtesy ReShawn Wilder.*

After a decade as a jazz mecca, the Paradise Theatre closed in 1951, a casualty of the fading popularity of the big bands. It took heroic measures by a preservation group to rescue the structure (and its irreplaceable acoustics) from demolition, but the effort was worth it. Now back to its original identity as home to the Detroit Symphony, its restoration job is one of the most admired in the country.

The Dakota Rathskeller, managed with tender-loving care by Karl Kurz, the grandson of its founders, still hosts its barrelhouse sing-alongs every weekend. The Blue Bird Inn hasn't hosted a jazz bill for years, but enthusiasts occasionally stop by to pay their respects. These pilgrims can hear live music seven nights a week at Baker's Keyboard Lounge, which, eight decades on, attracts people hungry for a taste of old-school intimacy and class. Then there are the Vanity and Grande Ballrooms, dilapidated but still standing, and the Crystal, now a luxury loft complex. With a little imagination as you stand in front of one of those buildings you can hear the whoops and shrieks of couples doing battle in a jitterbug contest.

Outside the city limits are more reminders of the war years. Oak Park's Quonset Hut Bar and Grill is no more, but the Victory Inn on Mound Road, near the tank arsenal grounds, remains very much in operation today.

Above: The Blue Bird Inn was a mecca for jazz fans. *Courtesy ReShawn Wilder.*

Below: The Vanity Ballroom on East Jefferson, once "Detroit's Most Beautiful Dance Rendezvous," 2015. *Courtesy ReShawn Wilder.*

Sign for "the Vic" at Mound and Twelve Mile, 2015. *Courtesy Steve Coddington.*

Alphonse and Mary DeLamielleure opened "the Vic" in 1946, and its success allowed them to raise ten children. One of them, Joe, became an NFL Hall of Famer with the Buffalo Bills, as a hand-painted mural at the entrance reminds us. The tavern serves burgers and drafts to a loyal clientele, and the sign out front brings to mind an era when Detroit was synonymous not with bankruptcy, dysfunction or decline, but with *victory*.

In downtown Ypsilanti, you can order a latte at B-24's Espresso Bar, a hangout for Eastern Michigan students glued to their smart phones and laptops. Down the street, you can indulge in the breakfast special at the Bomber Restaurant. Regulars watch as you survey the framed black-and-white photographs on the wall and the aircraft memorabilia hanging from the ceiling. One or two might have a story about a grandmother who was a spot-welder at The Run or an uncle who flew fighter missions in the Pacific when he was just a teenager.

Behind the counter are bright-colored posters of Rosie the Riveter, shirtsleeves rolled up, bicep flexed, red bandana pulled tightly around her head. "We Can Do It Again!" has been the rallying cry to save a section of Willow Run, owned since the 1950s by GM. In the summer of 2014, organizers announced that the $7.5 million needed to do that had been raised. Home to the volunteers of the Yankee Air Museum, it will bear witness to the people who worked there for many years to come.

Other efforts to keep the memories alive continue, in many places and on many fronts. The Michigan Military Technical and Historical Society operates a model small museum in Eastpointe, featuring locally built vehicles and all manner of other ordnance and artifacts from the war. "Chronicling Michigan in Defense of Democracy" is their motto. The Detroit Historical Museum's big exhibit on the homefront has won admirers of all ages with its display of war bond posters and ration coupon books, gas masks and other period items. In a mock-up living

B-24's Espresso Bar, Ypsilanti. *Courtesy Mike Wilhelm.*

Iconic Rosie image, used in a campaign to rescue a portion of Willow Run from the wrecking ball. *Courtesy Yankee Air Force.*

room, visitors can settle into the chair beside a cathedral radio and listen to FDR's "Arsenal of Democracy" fireside chat.

But the most important memorials have come in the words and example of the members of the war generation themselves. Their numbers are headed down to a precious few, but they are a hardy bunch, and many old soldiers still get into their uniforms to participate in anniversaries of Pearl Harbor and D-Day. With age, many end up in retirement communities or veterans' hospitals. Given a little help, others are able to stay in the homes they purchased so many years ago on the GI Bill.

As World War II recedes into the past, what can we say, finally, about how Americans, especially Detroiters, responded to its demands? The question defies pat answers. "War," Andy Rooney has written, recalling his days as a cub reporter for the *Stars and Stripes*, "encourages its citizens in the direction of excellence," and there is plenty of evidence to support this conclusion. Maya Angelou has described the sense of purpose and possibility she experienced during the war through the wide eyes of a teenager, the excitement of belonging and the chance to go beyond the small world into which she had been born. In her mind, this owed to the proximity to death everyone felt, "the air of collective displacement, the impermanence of life."

Geoffrey Perrett has expressed much the same sentiment about the war:

> For the vast majority of people, old and young, newcomers and old-timers, life was an exhilarating experience. There was plenty of money for almost everyone; there was a satisfying sensation of helping play an important part in the greatest, most worthwhile enterprise of the century; there was the chance to meet new people; there was the exposure to novel experiences. The gambling, the drinking and the overcrowding in the boomtowns often made life unpleasant. But the exhilaration was never destroyed, nor was the sense of importance.

Maury Klein offers a more temperate view. He reminds us:

> In every war, on every battlefield, there are heroes and cowards, stalwarts and shirkers, mainstays and misfits. The same holds just as true at home as at the front. Some people did their part, others did more than their share, and some did little if anything at all or tried to get what they could personally from the times. World War II differed from other wars in scale and scope but not in its diversity of human behavior and responses.

Old warriors recalling the past tend to smooth over or omit the painful parts, especially when speaking to someone who wasn't there. You can find them reminiscing together at the neighborhood VFW hall, Post No. 505, in the Mexican American section of southwest Detroit, for example. Eavesdroppers come away with new respect for the matter-of-fact humility they carried into their often grim jobs. Nothing "heroic" about it, they will tell you. To borrow a phrase from Rick Atkinson, these citizen-soldiers, plucked from a variety of circumstances and thrown into all kinds of impossible situations, did their best "to wage war *without liking it*."

Tuskegee Airman Charles McGee certainly approached his service that way. At a 2012 Detroit reunion of his fighter squadron—perhaps their last—a reporter asked him how he and his mates survived the war, considering the racism of the times and the dangers they faced on their combat missions. "We just wanted to get into the flying game, get through and get those wings," he replied, smiling and without a trace of drama. "We lived with it, but we didn't talk about it."

Because of the Red Tail pilots and many more like them, the pace of social change quickened after the war. In 1947, Jackie Robinson, an army

"Honor Peace." Exterior inscription on the Brodhead Naval Armory building on East Jefferson, 2015. *Courtesy ReShawn Wilder.*

lieutenant just back from the service, broke the color line in the national game, and the following year President Truman initiated the desegregation of the armed forces. Jim Crow as a legal system was on its way out. Similarly, millions of hardworking Rosies opened doors of opportunity, if not for themselves then for their daughters and granddaughters. Their efforts forced the country to live up to its promises and made sure the Four Freedoms meant something after all.

Even with the injustices perpetrated—by the good guys as well as the bad—and the waste and destruction visited on so many innocent lives, many good things came out of World War II. Its extraordinary challenges "encouraged Americans in the direction of excellence" and brought out the best in them. Like people across the nation, Detroiters dusted themselves off after being knocked down and worked together for the common good. These men and women don't need our mythologizing to burnish their achievements. But we owe it to them to celebrate and renew their spirit, for ourselves and for new generations living in a culture of forgetting.

The year 1945 was one of nail-biting excitement for fans of the Detroit Tigers. Known more for grit and tenacity than for talent, they were a surprise after several down seasons, still in contention as spring gave way to the dog days of summer. Hank Greenberg's return from the service on July 1 was a big lift. His home run that afternoon electrified the forty-seven thousand jammed into Briggs Stadium, and in the weeks to come he conjured enough of the old fire to keep championship dreams alive.

During his forty-seven months in the army air corps—the longest time away of any major leaguer during World War II—Captain Greenberg led a B-29 bomber squadron in the China-India-Burma theater, an assignment for which he earned four Battle Stars. Like a lot of vets, Hank didn't talk much about his experiences. To his mind, there was nothing special about the way he had done his duty, and lots of guys made sacrifices greater than his. Besides, dwelling on war stories would distract from challenges that demanded his full attention now. The most pressing was something all soldiers had to face, sooner or later: the need to turn the page and get on with civilian life.

Greenberg harbored no illusions about his abilities at this stage of his career. His once-mighty swing had lost velocity, his reflexes betrayed the effects of rust and age (he was an "old" thirty-four, the scouts said). Injuries nagged at him every time he took the field. There were still flashes of brilliance, like that welcome-back homer, but they were the exception now rather than the rule.

None of that mattered to Hank Greenberg. He was determined to reclaim his place in the game he loved and to have an impact as the Tigers rolled into their stretch drive.

September 30. Such light as there was that late afternoon of the final day of the season was fading fast as Detroit battled for a World Series berth, on the road at Sportsman's Park in St. Louis. Play had been suspended several times due to a bone-chilling mist of rain that made the infield a quagmire. Visibility was so poor the lead umpire considered calling the game without a decision. Six thousand hardy souls turned out to watch the Browns, already eliminated from the pennant chase, but their numbers dwindled as fog enveloped the field. The crack of the bat, the slap of the glove, the outfielders' chatter—all echoed eerily in the near-empty stadium.

Ninth Inning. Tigers' ace Hal Newhouser pitched well in late relief, but his team trailed as they came to bat for what would almost certainly be their last chance of the game. With two men on, Browns' manager Luke Sewell opted to load the bases to pitch to Greenberg. It was a kind of disrespect that would have been unthinkable earlier in his career, but now it was sound strategy, a matter of playing the percentages. Hank had been hobbled for weeks by a bad ankle, and he had been thrown out earlier that day on a base-running error. The former MVP was now so diminished, the thinking went, that even if he made contact, a routine throw to first would kill the Tiger rally.

Greenberg strode to the mud of the batter's box and—so the story goes—reassured the umpire he could see the ball "just fine," even as conditions continued to deteriorate. On the mound for St. Louis, Nelson Potter drew a bead, went into his wind-up and unloaded a pitch, outside. "Ball one!" barked the voice behind the plate. Back in Detroit, everyone was glued to a radio. With the count even, the pitcher went through his paces again and launched another throw.

Earlier in the game, Greenberg had noticed a hesitation in Potter's motion, a subtle tic telegraphing when he was about to deploy his signature screwball. Hammerin' Hank saw the hesitation now. His big frame was coiled in anticipation; he knew what was coming. The shoulders exploded with vintage speed as he drilled a shot out over the left field wall, just inside the foul pole. *A grand slam!*

Men became boys as they poured out of the visitors' dugout, shouting and jumping while they waited to receive the man of the hour. "By the time

A Curtiss P-40 Warhawk soars over downtown. Fighter planes tearing across the sky were a common sight during World War II. *Courtesy Selfridge Air Museum.*

Hank reached home plate, he was caught up in a maelstrom of humanity, which was every Tiger on the team," the *Free Press* said the next morning. "He was hugged and roughed up and kissed and pummeled."

Fans in the Motor City—"and who *wasn't* a Tiger fan Sunday?"—erupted in like fashion. The manager at the Telenews theater downtown said that his customers made more of a ruckus over this event than they had when the Japanese surrender flashed across the lobby teletype six weeks earlier. In the basement radio lounge, "several happy listeners seized usherettes and gave them resounding kisses."

Greenberg took his victory lap with majestic deliberation, savoring the moment in all its grandeur. No doubt among the thoughts running through his head as he rounded the bases in that cold, miserable twilight, in front of all those empty seats, was one he remembered from the long-ago days before the war: "I just hit another one against Hitler!"

The team held on for the win, and the second game of a scheduled double-header was canceled. Owner Walter Briggs telephoned his

Storefront across from General George S. Patton Park, Wildemere and Vernor Avenue, 2015. *Photo by Gregory Sumner*.

congratulations and told the players to enjoy the train ride home, which he christened the Victory Special. The food and drinks were on him. When the American League champs pulled into Michigan Central, thousands of the faithful were there to greet them. Hammerin' Hank would deliver again in the World Series, smashing two homers to lead his team over the Chicago Cubs in seven.

It was all richly symbolic, a fitting coda to a time of sweet victory for the citizens of Detroit that could not have been better scripted by Hollywood. Like the "miraculous" job they had done to back up FDR's promise of an Arsenal of Democracy, the baseball star's larger-than-life heroics would soon become the stuff of legend. Maybe other vets would take comfort from his example, as they made *their* way back from the war.

Like the city he represented, and when it counted most, Hank Greenberg was slaying dragons, sending messages, *forging thunderbolts*.

SELECTED BIBLIOGRAPHY

Abraham, Nabeel, and Andrew Shryock, eds. *Arab Detroit: From Margin to Mainstream*. Detroit: Wayne State University Press, 2000.

Atkinson, Rick. *The Day of Battle: The War in Sicily and Italy, 1943–44*. New York: Henry Holt, 2007.

Austin, Dan. *Forgotten Detroit Landmarks*. Charleston, SC: The History Press, 2012.

Baime, A.J. *The Arsenal of Democracy: FDR, Detroit, and an Epic Quest to Arm America at War*. New York: Houghton Mifflin Harcourt, 2014.

Bjorn, Lars. *Before Motown: A History of Jazz in Detroit, 1920–60*. Ann Arbor: University of Michigan Press, 2001.

Blum, John Morton. *V Was for Victory: Politics and Culture during World War II*. New York: Harcourt Brace & Company, 1976.

Francis, Charles E., and Adolph Caso. *The Tuskegee Airmen: The Men Who Changed a Nation*. Boston: Branden Books, 1997.

Gluck, Sherna Berger. *Rosie the Riveter Revisited: Women, the War, and Social Change*. New York: Penguin, 1988.

Goodwin, Doris Kearns. *No Ordinary Time: Franklin and Eleanor Roosevelt and the Home Front in World War II*. New York: Simon & Schuster, 1994.

Hyde, Charles. *Arsenal of Democracy: The American Automobile Industry in World War II*. Detroit: Wayne State University, 2013.

Lingeman, Richard. *Don't You Know There's a War On?: The American Home Front*. New York: G.P. Putnam's Sons, 2003.

Matuz, Roger. *Albert Kahn, Master Builder*. Detroit: Wayne State University Press, 2002.

Perrett, Geoffrey. *Days of Sadness, Years of Triumph: The American People, 1939–1945*. Madison: University of Wisconsin Press, 1973.

Rosengren, John. *Hank Greenberg: The Hero of Heroes*. New York: Penguin, 2013.

Terkel, Studs. *The Good War: An Oral History of World War II*. New York: The New Press, 1984.

INDEX

A

Angelou, Maya 17, 149
An Open Letter on Race Hatred 102
"Avenue of Fashion" 106
Avery, Marjorie 69

B

B-24's Espresso Bar 147
Baker's Keyboard Lounge 82, 145
Belle Isle 10, 58, 66, 82, 93, 100, 131
Better Made potato chips 110, 111
black market 86, 106, 108
"Bloody Monday" 97
Blue Bird Inn 82, 145
Bob-lo Island 117
"Bomber City" 46, 47
Briggs Stadium 119, 122, 143, 151
Brodhead Naval Armory 66, 96, 150

C

Churchill, Winston 12, 17, 128
civil defense 61, 62, 63
Coughlin, Charles 10, 95, 120
Cunningham's Drugs 77, 110, 116

D

Dakota Inn Rathskeller 93, 145
Davison freeway 51
Detroit Symphony Orchestra 82, 83, 145
"Double Victory" 78, 103

F

Faygo 110
"Fire Balloons" 134
Ford, Edsel 31, 32, 35, 36, 38, 138
Ford, Henry 21, 25, 28, 30, 31, 32, 35, 47, 48, 120, 138
Ford, Henry, II 38
Fort Wayne 66
Four Freedoms 60, 108, 116, 151

G

Goering, Herman 23, 106
Gordy, Berry 84
Graystone Ballroom 83, 84
Greenberg, Hank 120, 121, 122, 151, 152, 153, 154
Green Hornet 115

H

"Hamtramck Mama" 85
Hoffa, Jimmy 53
Hudson's department store 60, 106, 107, 139

J

Jam Handy 26
Jeffries, Edward 81, 97, 100

K

Kahn, Albert 25, 27, 30
Knudson, William 12, 24, 25
Koppitz's "Victory Beer" 111, 112

L

LaGuardia, Fiorello 63
Levine, Philip 64
Lindbergh, Charles 10, 31, 32, 35, 140
Lone Ranger 115, 116
Louis, Joe 22, 66, 76, 83, 118, 119, 121

M

Mauldin, Bill 68
Michigan Central 15, 135, 144, 154
Monroe, Rose Will 43, 136
Moody, Frank 57, 58, 76, 78
Murphy, Frank 131, 133
Murrow, Edward R. 72

N

Naff, Alixa 98, 99, 100, 140
Nancy Brown Peace Carillon 10
Navin Field Grounds Crew 143
Newhouser, Hal 123, 152

O

Olympia Stadium 103, 119, 143
"Optimistic Olivers" 137

P

Packard Motor Car Company 25, 42, 96, 138, 140
Paradise Theatre 83, 145
Paradise Valley 22, 84, 96, 100, 130, 139
Pewabic Pottery 66
Pyle, Ernie 68, 69, 90

R

Redford Theatre 88, 93, 144
Reuther, Walter 17, 30, 52
Rockwell, Norman 44, 45, 52
Roosevelt, Eleanor 14, 33, 36, 42, 76, 99, 102
Roosevelt, Franklin D. 9, 10, 11, 23, 24, 33, 37, 60, 67, 76, 86, 92, 93, 100, 120, 123, 127, 128, 154
Rosie the Riveter 39, 40, 41, 43, 44, 45, 85, 115, 116, 136, 137, 147, 151

S

Slovik, Eddie 143
Sojourner Truth homes 95
Sorensen, Charles 30, 31, 35, 36
Stalin, Joseph 17, 138
Stephan, Max 93

T

Telenews Theater 71, 72, 74, 144, 153
Truman, Harry 32, 128, 129, 151
Turner, Joe 119, 144
Tuskegee Airmen 57, 76, 150

U

University of Detroit 118, 131, 132, 136
USS *Detroit* 127, 138

V

Vanity Ballroom 82, 83, 145, 146
Vernor's 84, 110
V-Girls 117
Victory Gardens 18, 84, 109

Victory Inn 145
Victory Speed Limit 105

W

Warren Tank Arsenal 35, 51, 138, 145
Willow Run 28, 30, 31, 32, 35, 37, 38,
        39, 42, 43, 45, 47, 48, 51, 66,
        116, 136, 138, 140, 147
Windsor, Canada 21, 25, 93, 119
WPA *Guide to Michigan* 21, 120

Y

Yamamoto, Isoroku 16, 23
Yankee Air Museum 45, 147

Z

Zoot suits 94, 107

ABOUT THE AUTHOR

Gregory D. Sumner, JD, PhD, is co-chair of history at the University of Detroit Mercy, where he has taught since 1993. He holds a doctorate in American history from Indiana University and is the author of *Dwight Macdonald and the Politics Circle* and *Unstuck in Time: A Journey through Kurt Vonnegut's Life and Novels*. Sumner has been awarded fellowships by the National Endowment for the Humanities and has twice been William J. Fulbright Senior Lecturer at the Université di Roma Tre.